Goodbye Fear, Hello Destiny!

Tamara Mitchell-Davis

Goodbye Fear, Hello Destiny!

Tamara Mitchell-Davis

Tamara Mitchell-Davis
2018

Goodbye Fear, Hello Destiny!

ISBN 978-1-7328270-0-4

Edited by Renee Y. Reliford
books531@comcast.net

Cover design by Linkz Media
www.linkzmedia.com

Cover and back photo by LMG Photography
www.lesliegomezphotography.com

To contact Tamara Mitchell-Davis
Tmdavis860@gmail.com
www.tamaramdavis.com

Follow on Instagram @GoalGetter860

Follow on Facebook https://www.facebook.com/GoalGetter860/

First Printing: 2018

Other books published by Author
#GoalGetter: Strategies for Overcoming Life's Challenges
Published 2017

Goodbye Fear, Hello Destiny!

Tamara Mitchell-Davis

DEDICATION

I dedicate this book to my amazing mother Carolynn -- whom I love beyond any words. You were my first teacher in turning lemons into lemonade. Thank you for inspiring me and loving me unconditionally at ALL times. I feel honored to call you my Mother.

TABLE OF CONTENTS

FOREWORD

About two years ago, a mutual friend sent me an email, introducing me to someone who worked in education that in her words, "I had to meet!" We arranged to connect at a local tea shop for about an hour at the end of the day, squeezing in a brief moment between events that we each were rushing to accommodate. This individual was very humble, even a little nervous. She sat across from me with anticipation; she had heard a lot about me -- in particular, my career trajectory and community involvement. At the end of a long work day, with more events to come, we opted for a cocktail and a shared appetizer -- not too sure if the evening events would provide us any food. We talked about our lives - careers, children, our aspirations. We didn't talk about writing though; nor was she aware that I had written a book myself. But mine has been a bit of a dream deferred; I just couldn't seem to get on track with moving it forward! A connection was made and from that moment forward, our paths continued to cross. Months later when Tamara let me know that she was completing a book, I knew that our connection was no accident.

For far too long, women have shouldered the burdens of absolutely everyone and everything! We wear those broad shoulders as a badge of honor. We hold back our tears or allow them to fall only when in the shower, where they become one with the drops of water and quickly disappear down the drain. We go to extremes when things go wrong; we even throw our own pity party. We celebrate others, while keeping our hands to the plow. We sacrifice, putting our own dreams on the back burner. Boy, we think we can do it all! Often times, we hold all of that in - our disappointments, struggles, fears -- and our dreams. We think that no one will understand or worse that someone will convince us that our dreams cannot come true!

As a working mom, I know all too well the struggle of the oft illusive work life balance. I've also regularly set goals for myself and yet in many instances, I have had to put my own pursuits on the back burner when life has "happened".

It is those life experiences from which Tamara established her own unique balance of practical and inspirational in her first book, #GoalGetter. Her experiences were relatable and real. Her new book, *Goodbye Fear, Hello Destiny*, takes those initial learnings and uses them to shape a road map for women and men alike to follow. It wasn't easy, and it took some time for her first book to come to fruition. All of life's twists and turns stood in the way and just like many of us, our goals and dreams can get just a little off track. But now Tamara is on fire!

A daughter, wife, mother, education advocate, community leader and friend, Tamara is living her life out loud!! On the heels of instant success with #GoalGetter, *Goodbye Fear, Hello Destiny* is proof positive that Tamara has made it a priority to listen to the musings of her heart; the whispers that have been telling her "YES, YOU CAN", all along. Her perseverance has paid off, not only in her own success, but in the knowledge that our blessings are not simply our own. With each and every one of you that reads this book, the hard times, challenges, barriers and delayed victories, have proven to be well worth it. When Tamara shared her plans with me about this project, I was humbled, in awe and so proud that she was preparing to birth yet another dream into reality! I'm inspired by her words and even more inspired by her actions. This book symbolizes more than just another goal achieved for Tamara; it's a movement for us all!

Tamara encourages us to make our dreams a reality and put ourselves first and she also shows us how to do it! Join the movement, friends! Allow *Goodbye Fear, Hello Destiny* to position you to revisit and reach your goals, embrace your own potential, silence the naysayers, and soar into your destiny!

Joelle A. Murchison
Accomplished Executive, Diversity & Inclusion Champion and Founder and Principal, ExecMommy
info@execmommy.org
www.execmommy.org
FB Twitter IG @execmommy

INTRODUCTION

As I started writing this book, I was thinking about the framework and purpose it would serve. I wanted it to be a source of inspiration, motivation, and self-reflection to encourage others to live outside of the box and bubble that our thoughts and, sometimes, people may put or keep us in.

Too often I found myself asking the same questions over and over again …

Who am I?

What is my purpose?

What kind of legacy will I leave behind?

How do I make sense of this life?

What does "winning" actually mean?

Where do I go from here?

and the ultimate…..Why?

Who, What, How, Where, When, and Why? These are questions that play constantly in my head like a broken record. For the most part, I am convinced that I am an "over thinker" and borderline perfectionist (squirmish grin). I hear stories all the time about risk takers who "jumped" and took chances without any hesitation because thinking TOO much stifled their movement. For me, ideas would flood my brain to the tenth degree but because I had to process every miniscule thought, my actions were at a standstill (fear). I would have dreams, wake up, write the information down and know in my heart what to do but I wasn't too great at implementation and risk taking. Instead, I became an expert at planning only. I would plan everything from beginning to end and then beginning again. I would include a Plan B and Plan C and then go back to the original plan and rework it. It was a never ending cycle as I strived to perfect that which needed no perfection. I would like to believe it was me using caution, however, I know it was fear that kept me playing it safe.

I once allowed fear of the unknown and fear of failure to cripple me to a place where I questioned EVERYTHING and did not act on ANYTHING. I've learned that challenges and obstacles have helped me to grow but I didn't always see it this way. I would be so frustrated with myself because I would stand on the edge of a decision that I knew I wanted and needed to make but I was afraid to let go and jump. My daughters were depending on me so it wasn't easy for me to play the risk game.

Fast forward to now. Although I have stumbled along the way, there is absolutely nothing wrong with weighing the pros and cons before making a decision. It's when it totally consumes you day and night with no actions behind it that it may potentially become a problem. At least this was my situation. Before, I felt guilty for not always being quick on my feet and moving swiftly. Some people might call this indecisiveness but I thought I was being extremely careful and cautious with my thoughts and actions. I had to deal with the root as to why it would take me so long to make a decision and act. Was it fear, doubt, time constraints or just procrastination? Quickly, I discovered two things about myself that alluded to the possibility of why I was not a risk taker.

One: During my childhood, I experienced various situations that had me living in a state of uncertainty: evictions, parental substance abuse, co-dependency, drive-by shootings, drug infested housing project, death of close friends, low self-esteem, loss of friendships, abandonment, and lack of trust in others, to name a few.

Two: Entering "my" adulthood at the age of 17, I dealt with stressors previously mentioned compounded with verbal and, sometimes, physical abuse, manipulative relationships, single parenting, divorce, and the weight of survival as I journeyed through different stages and phases of my life.

Because I never wanted to end up in the same circumstance that I was exposed to and eventually left, I was paralyzed and paranoid about making decisions that could put me back in any one of the situations previously referenced. I had started operating out of fear and playing it as safe as possible while trying to live in my "normal" state of uncertainty. Sound crazy? Let me further clarify.

For example, if as a child I experienced multiple evictions, once I became a parent, my mindset was totally fixated on doing what I could so that my children would never experience what I had gone through. This impacted work, school and even relationships. Because I was once in an abusive relationship, I became "tough" and built a wall up to avoid people from hurting me and really getting close to me.

Playing it "safe" was my way of controlling any situation to avoid a negative outcome. Because I never wanted to end up in those situations again, I became very cautious about how I moved, what I said, and who I dealt with. I took less risk and operated in survival mode for a long time. In hindsight (and now as an experienced woman), those situations, circumstances and experiences were lessons that made me wiser and the woman I am today. I can't and I won't discredit who I am and what I have experienced nor am I ashamed of my past. As I dissected it a bit more, I also realized that I lacked confidence in my own abilities and capabilities. When you lack confidence you may tend to also operate in fear. Fear is something that most people struggle with: *fear of failure, fear of the unknown, fear of success, fear of death, fear of being alone, fear of public speaking, fear itself, and the list continues.* But what is FEAR? False Evidence Appearing Real? Fear keeps so many people bound, in situations much longer than they should be, confused, and afraid. Does any of this resonate with you?

Often, we are told that we need to have a plan and I am a strong advocate in setting goals and having a plan. Hence, my first book *#GoalGetter: Strategies for Overcoming Life's Challenges.* We are also led to believe that if we travel without a route in mind or map in hand, we'll end up at a dead end. At least this was my truth and what I was taught coming up and learned along the way. I was caught on the hamster wheel spinning around and around. What I have come to realize is that you don't need to have it all figured out and there is no such thing as perfection. Sometimes getting lost is a part of the divine plan which can lead to the most beautiful destinations that you never knew existed.

Getting lost breeds awareness and self-discovery. Think about what you do when you are lost or unsure about something. You either use technology for quick results, do some investigating to figure it out OR you get assistance from someone to help you get back on the "right" road.

When it becomes survival mode, you might start lighting smoke signals, getting creative, resourceful, and pulling from strength you never knew existed.

To avoid this continuous cycle, I had to intentionally acknowledge what was going on within and around me. There were times when I had to slow down the hamster wheel in order to jump off and then there were times when I just had to take the leap of faith being unsure of where I would land. It was a process though and it did not happen overnight.

Thank God I know what I am capable of now. However, then I felt that I had to have everything figured out before I could make any decision because I was uncertain of the outcome, be it positive or negative. I had to call out the Fear and learn to do things while being afraid.

We all have our own journey and we must be willing to learn during trials, tribulations, obstacles and even victories. My prayer is that this book will inspire you to live with purpose, passion, and authenticity as you face your fears while in pursuit of your dreams.

Goodbye Fear, Hello Destiny!

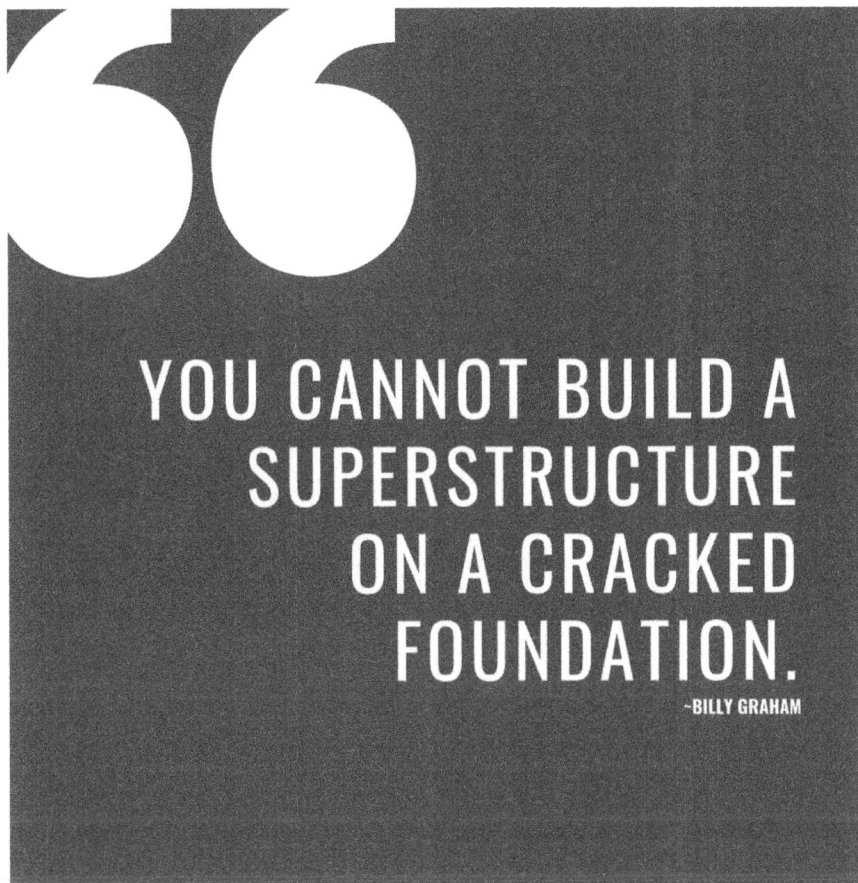

YOU CANNOT BUILD A
SUPERSTRUCTURE
ON A CRACKED
FOUNDATION.
~BILLY GRAHAM

BUILD YOUR FOUNDATION

Rock bottom became the solid foundation
on which I rebuilt my life.
J.K. Rowling

I've shared with you some initial thoughts about my challenges and how I have processed information for quite some time. I've shared my "reasoning" as to how I ended up that way and how it has hindered me in the past. I have been more intentional in identifying my shortcomings in order to create a better me and work toward self-improvement and growth. If you are content with where you are or how things are going then there is no need to change. However, if you know of an area that needs improvement then I urge you to do some self-reflecting to determine the root cause of the issue. We can't confront or change things we don't know or identify with.

As defined by Merriam-Webster dictionary, foundation is the basis upon which something stands or is supported; an underlying base or support. The purpose of a foundation is to hold up or hold together the structure that rest above it. If the foundation is secure and properly built, it can withstand various acts of mother nature and, therefore, things and people inside are kept safe. Foundation holds up a house. Any mistakes you make in building the foundation will only get worse or have a negative impact as you go up. How can we relate this to our personal self?

During childhood one may have experienced or been exposed to situations or circumstances that affected the foundation. As a child, someone put a bill in your name and never paid it or stole your "identify". This affected your credit score and credit history before you became of age to even know what credit is. Or, perhaps, someone always told you to be quiet, shut up or speak when spoken to. As you grew, your voice became silent and now you keep your thoughts, ideas, and opinions to yourself. Or, here is another one....being raised by a single parent, foster parent or a "child" raising another child and as they grew in age and maturity, lacked trust with people and struggled with abandonment issues. Some might think that when you leave childhood and grow into adulthood you leave ALL the memories, interactions and experiences behind. We might forget some things but the same person that was a child has now evolved into an adult. More than likely, fear, insecurities, those same thoughts, and doubt went right along with them playing itself out in other ways. It's not until we recognize it that we are able to face it and actually deal with it.

When writing this book, I surveyed several groups of people and the common fears they expressed were fear of the unknown, fear of failure, fear of abandonment, and fear of public speaking. The same fears I struggled with. Fear is an emotion (not a person) that often times causes a racing heart, fast breathing, and sweaty hands. This emotion holds millions of people back from taking risks, growing, developing, and becoming the best version of themselves. Fear causes you to second guess your goals, ambitions, purpose and will definitely prevent you from taking action. What I want you to know and understand is that *FEAR* is normal and most struggle with it in some way, shape, or form. The key is to not let fear hold you back and prevent you from taking action and going after what you want and desire in your life. As you read, I will be referencing grace and grit sporadically throughout the book. To minimize any confusion and maximize common understanding for foundational purposes, I have also shared Webster's dictionary of both words:

Grace has several meanings including, (1) it is seen and acknowledged throughout the Bible as unmerited mercy from God; (2) an act of kindness that we extend to others; (3) a short prayer at a meal asking a blessing or giving thanks; (4) a charming or attractive trait or characteristic; (5) the quality or state of being considerate or thoughtful, (6) an allowance of time after a debt or bill has become payable granted to the debtor before suit can be brought against him or her or penalty applied; (7) courteous goodwill.

As with grace, grit has several meanings as well. (1) sand, gravel; (2) the structure of a stone that adapts it to grinding; (3) the size of abrasive particles usually expressed as their mesh; (4) firmness of mind or spirit; unyielding courage in the face of hardship or danger; (5) strength of character; (6) clenching one's teeth.

Do any of the definitions immediately resonate with you? In both definitions, I found traces of my character and who I have become. The fear may have been present but I found a way to tiptoe around it and cry my way through it. Ultimately, it produced *strength, courage, perseverance, and ambition* without me even knowing it. Think about a situation you were in that provoked the emotion of fear. There was no turning back and you had to do it even in fear. In the end, did that experience produce more fear or was it a sense of accomplishment? How did you feel when it was all said and done? Was it a sense of relief? If you had to do it over, you may be afraid again, but now you can reflect on the previous experience and say to yourself…. *"If I did it once, I can do it again"*. And, 9 times out of 10, most likely YOU CAN! We are much stronger than what we give ourselves credit for.

GRIT IS PASSION FOR PERSEVERANCE FOR VERY LONG TERM GOALS. GRIT IS HAVING STAMINA. GRIT IS STICKING WITH YOUR FUTURE, DAY IN AND DAY OUT-- NOT JUST FOR A DAY, NOT JUST FOR A MONTH, BUT FOR YEARS-- TO MAKE THAT FUTURE REALITY.

-ANGELA LEE DUCKWORTH

VULNERABILITY

Never Ever Ever Give Up On Your Dream

It takes a lot of courage and humility to be transparent and vulnerable. This is not to say and encourage anyone to walk around yelling or toting a sign that says…"Hey look at me, I am transparent and vulnerable." Let me repeat that again…This is not to encourage anyone to walk around with a transparent and vulnerable mantra. There is a time and place for everything. Within reason, we must determine when the time and place is right to be transparent and vulnerable. Some situations do not create the platform to be open and exposed as much as we would like to be so please use wisdom when doing so. Here are my transparent and vulnerable moments. I am ok with sharing this openly because for me it was a learning experience.

Lesson 1: When I released my first book, #GoalGetter; Strategies to Overcome Life's Challenges, I had no clue about everything it took to write a book, self-publish and market it because this was my first time. It was a long process (years) for me to finish the book because I kept starting, stopping, starting again and became discouraged along the way. I had no one to share my ideas with. I shared that I was writing a book with people who were close to me, but I did not share the nuts, bolts and framework of the book. Most were quite surprised when I actually self-published because I had been talking about it but there was no evidence of actually working on it to bring it to fruition. The truth of the matter – I was unsure of myself. I was sharing information in the book that had been buried for some time. Writing the book was a form of therapy as I was able to face some of the hardcore situations that kept me boxed in (my thoughts), struggling with doubt (circumstances), reliving old pain and hurt (regret), and kept me bound (choices I had made).

The book was the reintroduction to events and incidents that I encountered from childhood into adulthood and strategies that worked for me to overcome them emotionally, mentally, and spiritually. The stories were factual so there were people that I had to leave nameless for privacy sake. I am excited and proud of this accomplishment but through it all and even as I write now, I can't help but question myself if I could have gone a little deeper. If it fulfilled its purpose?. Did it leave an impact on each reader and anyone who supported the work? What could I have done differently? This is a part of my self-reflective moments as I strive to improve myself daily. Some may identify with it and for some the process may be slightly different.

Lesson 2: When I considered the book cover, I questioned whether or not to put my picture on the front. I did not want my picture (brown female) to deter anyone from reading the narrative. All kinds of questions flooded my mind: Is it relatable? Is it a good read? Who would want to hear "my" story? I considered my audience and was a bit nervous and apprehensive about putting myself out there like that. Then I questioned myself more. Did my many wonderings stem from a place of doubt, fear and embarrassment? The bottom line - I had nothing to be embarrassed about. We all have our own "story" of life. Some things are relatable and some are unique. I am the expert of MY life and you are the expert of yours. Although I opted not to go with my picture on the cover of the book, I allowed the reader to get a snapshot through shared photos of various moments in my life and shared examples of strength and perseverance.

Lesson 3: I do not consider myself to be the most experienced and technologically advanced person (I am learning as I go). So I thought my work was done because I finally completed my book when in all actuality, the work had just begun. Again, I had no clue about this new world I was venturing into. I knew I wanted to write and share my story. I knew I wanted to publish. I knew Microsoft Word but there were other things that took more time to figure out: hiring an editor, hiring someone to create my book cover, planning a book release, coordinating a book tour, adding merchandise that aligned with my book, facing the challenges that I would soon encounter and learning from mistakes along the way. These were all fears that I had to face, deal with, and overcome.

It is so easy to take a picture, upload it to Facebook and Instagram and make things look glamourous to show what you are doing to build your brand. There is so much work that goes on behind the scenes. There were times when I reached out to people for guidance and received no help. Because of that, I felt inadequate. People are quick to ask for help, receive it and then don't return the courtesy. Some people want you to do well but not better than them. The people I thought would be supportive weren't and I even learned valuable lessons even in those experiences.

So how does this relate to grace and grit? Glad you asked. ☺

There is absolutely nothing wrong with figuring it out. It may take a bit longer (as it did for me) but the knowledge received by me having to figure it out on my own and the lessons I learned through the process are priceless. Does it get frustrating at times? Can it be overwhelming? Will you question the value of your project or even the ideas you envisioned? Absolutely! But what I must tell you is that if you don't believe in your work then no one else will. If you don't value it then you can't expect others to. If you don't talk about it then no one will hear it.

For me, it all aligned but I had to stay the course. I had to find a way to push through my wonderings and fear. Once you know better, you do better. You have to represent your own brand and toot your own horn *(self-promote)*. It is not being conceited and arrogant; it is believing so much in yourself that even if you encounter people who don't support you, you humbly push pass them and identify those who will. When and if you should face any challenging situations, you see the challenge as an opportunity to assess where you are in order to determine your course of action and keep pressing forward.

I made reference to people I intentionally sought for assistance that were either not willing to help or did not believe in what I had to offer. I was seeking help from the wrong people, because there were a few people who I never considered asking but ironically they showed up and asked me what they could do to assist me. Or they would pour into me through prayer and shared their own nuggets of wisdom to help me. I did not realize this until later because I was expecting the support and assistance to come from specific people. Thankfully, I kept moving in spite of my feelings and disappointments.

Once I started step one, the next step automatically revealed itself in order for me to work on step two. Who I thought or expected to assist didn't and either I figured it out on my own or divine intervention occurred. I ended up

30

where I was supposed to be at the time I was supposed to be there. I met who I was supposed to connect with in order to move my project to the next phase. I was learning how to fish rather than sit at a table eating food that was already prepared for me. When you learn how to fish, you will never go hungry because you will figure it out which equips you with so much information and knowledge that you have no choice but to grow if you choose. I had to get out of my own way and not worry about who was not willing to help me and figure out *how to help myself.*

For example, I couldn't start the editing process if I didn't have a manuscript to edit. One step preceded the next and although I did not know who, what, where, why, and how the next step was supposed to be or go, I had to start somewhere and with something to even work with. You see, it took me so long to get it done because I initially thought I had to have it all figured out when that was not the case. I just needed to start. It took me so long to get it done because I lacked the confidence and was embarrassed by some of the trials and tribulations that I had encountered early on.

Many times we get discouraged if the "right" people do not support or if everything isn't revealed to us immediately. Think of a portrait. I am sure the artist had a picture in mind but he or she had to first prepare with the necessary tools and supplies in order to start painting. Merely thinking about it didn't yield any results. The artist had to pick up the paint brush and actually begin putting the paint on a canvas to create the masterpiece.

What have you been considering or even started doing but have put off because you didn't have the "right" people in your corner or you did not have it all figured out? PAUSE

HERE AND REALLY THINK ABOUT AND RESPOND TO
THAT QUESTION....

*What have you been considering or even started doing but
have put off because you didn't have the "right" people in
your corner or you did not have it all figured out?*

_____

_____

_____

In order to get to the next step you must first START. I
was transparent and vulnerable in my process because I
acknowledged that I did not know it all. I did not have all
the answers. I was honest with myself first and then sought
what I considered to be "help" in areas of weakness and
challenges. In spite of not receiving assistance or guidance
when requested, I still had a made up mind. As I stated
earlier, use wisdom when being transparent and vulnerable.
If you need help, ask someone who can help you. *A closed
mouth doesn't get fed.*

Through experiences, lack of support, the word "NO"
and even times of discouragement, I can look back and see
how grace and grit were evident and exercised. Through it
all, I remained focused. I may have fallen off course from
time to time but I found my way back and ended up right
where I was supposed to be.

I know it is easier said than done but try not to be so
stressed because everything does not fall into place as you
hoped or you are not where you wanted to be at this
particular time. There is no time like the PRESENT to start
and restart again. We get worked up about things we have
no control over and about people who don't support us. If

we believe that everything happens for a reason, then we may need to shift our thinking to know that we are right where we are supposed to be at this particular stage in life. People will show up and when opportunities don't come, make them.

Besides, we don't know it to be any different. We cannot go back and undo what is already done. We can focus on where we are right now and start, or in some cases, restart. Once we start or re-start, the next step will reveal itself. I am a witness that you don't need to have it all figured out. This was my hurdle for so long so learn from my mistake.

Trust the process. Trust your intuition. *Believe in yourself and stay focused!*

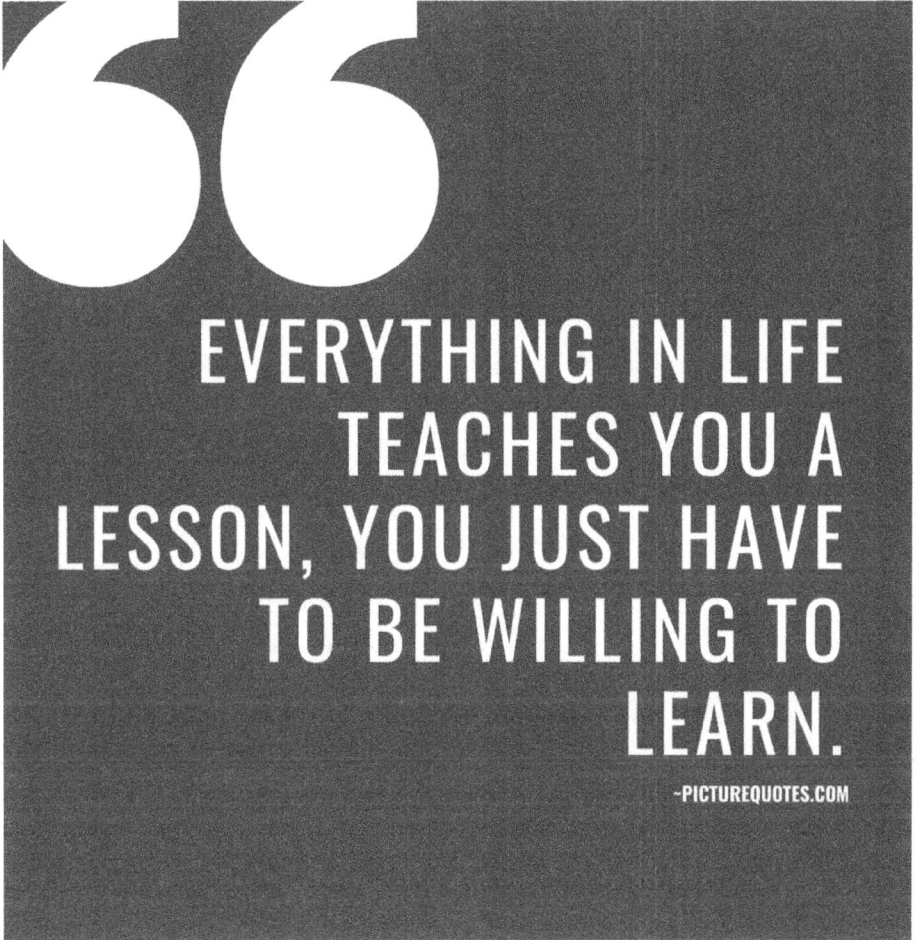

EVERYTHING IN LIFE TEACHES YOU A LESSON, YOU JUST HAVE TO BE WILLING TO LEARN.

-PICTUREQUOTES.COM

A LESSON CAN BE A BLESSING

Every encounter we have had in life or will face will be a lesson one way or another. The question is ....are you willing to learn?

Right after high school, I was accepted into a local university and scheduled to begin in the fall. I started at the university and then due to finances, pregnancy, and other circumstances, I ended up not returning. I shared a jist of the story in the #GoalGetter book. I had my daughter and began working a temporary work assignment with a staffing agency. I remember when I was about 21 years old with a young child, I landed what I considered to be a great full-time, union status job opportunity. I had great benefits and a good salary for my age. I was also living in my own apartment, had joined a credit union, purchased a "hoopty" which means "old car" and I was taking care of my responsibilities as a single parent. Needless to say, I was feeling good about myself.

I don't know if this was a threat to my supervisor or if other factors came into play. I was the youngest in the department. I was smart, quick and the work that took staff members to get done in months' time, I was breezing through in weeks. I was being recognized for my work by people outside of the department. And then I started to feel uncomfortable. Peers in the department were telling me what was said about me on my days off and who said it. I shared this with my mother and went to a supervisor I trusted who worked in another department and both of them advised me to start "documenting" everything and to maintain my professionalism. And so, I did. I knew about professionalism early on. I was a participant in programs while in high school that groomed me for the workplace. I had internships as well so I knew how to conduct myself and the importance of customer service.

As for documenting, I kept my own log of case notes from the time I arrived, the work flow and staff encounters. I had all the documentation in a folder should I ever need it. Why else would my mom or the other supervisor advise me to document?

To provide some context, the manager in my department was an African American older woman. I admired her for making it to her position and thought I could learn from her. It was rare to see women of color in management. My view of her soon changed. I remember clearly being called into her office as soon as I had arrived to work. She sat me down and basically said she knew who my family members were and that she had some conflict with one in particular. She went on to give me a spiel about the difference in being fired versus resigning from a position. She had no grounds to fire me based on association but told me that the work environment was now awkward for her and that if I resigned, I would be eligible for future employment opportunities. Honestly, I sat there shocked, stunned, in disbelief and in tears. I tried to wrap my head around what was happening. Be fired or work somewhere else is all I could think about. I had a baby to feed and rent to pay. I had no clue about unions although I was a member of one. Of course, I would have preferred to step out of the office, call my mother and ask if this could happen. I wanted to know my rights. I wanted to hurt the manager for even putting me in this situation but all I kept thinking about was my baby and survival. Be fired and tarnish my record or work somewhere else? She even had the resignation letter typed and on her desk waiting for a signature. "Be fired, have my record tarnished or work somewhere else", kept playing in my head. I am not trying to dismiss the fact that perhaps I should have taken the time to understand my rights but when put in hostile situations, we may not always think and react clearly.

I signed the letter, gathered my belongings, left the office and called my mother sobbing and explaining to her what had occurred. She directed me to go talk to the union representative before I left the building and so I did. I went to the union representative within an hour's time and shared what had occurred. I presented the letter and used the exact words my mother had given me...FORCED RESIGNATION. I even told the union representative that I had talked with another supervisor in a different department and started documenting incidents. I was informed by the union representative that because I had signed the letter, that was my consent. I should not have signed the letter and came straight to see them. Again, I was in tears. Of course, if I had known that then, I would not have reacted in that same manner. I was hurt and angry. I felt betrayed, bamboozled and manipulated and there was nothing I could do about it. I had paid into a union that did not help me in the end. I had given my time, talent and energy to a department that stripped me of confidence and livelihood. This was no reflection on the organization as a whole. This was purely individual agendas and motives.

So when I hear that people may have reacted to a particular situation under pressure without knowing better, I tend to believe them. Why? Because it happened to me. When I have shared this story, I received all kinds of suggestions as to how I could have addressed the situation differently. Now I know. When I know better I can do better. However, I am not trying to say that all 21 year olds are naïve and clueless. I admit looking back, I probably should have walked out and filed a complaint. I just wasn't aware of my rights and how to react in that manner. That was the first time I had experienced such treatment. Here is the kicker; one of the women in the department who was gossiping about me was a relative of my sibling. She considered me her niece and I considered her my aunt. In a nutshell, what I am trying to say is that some learning comes from experience. The situation definitely taught me to ask more questions and investigate before I commit to something, especially decisions that are life altering. It gave me a huge lesson on family as you can imagine.

For anyone who knows me, perhaps, you can understand now why loyalty means so much to me. There are certain things I just wouldn't expect family, friends and anyone who has my best interest at heart to do. There should be an understanding of trustworthiness, allegiance, dependability, and faithfulness when it comes to individuals who "claim" to be close to you. Family and friends, in particular. When I see anything contrary to that and feel that I cannot trust a person or I have to question loyalty, intentions and agenda, distance will intervene.

We form our values and belief system through our upbringing. We react to people and situations based on experiences that we have encountered. When people show you who they are...believe them. That is a cliché that has been around for some time now.

In order to guard my heart, my defense mechanism is to leave them alone. I can't say or encourage you to do the same. This was my way of processing things and protecting myself. I cannot be open and honest with someone I knowingly cannot trust. I cannot have people around me who knowingly reveal that they are against me. It's like giving someone a weapon to hurt you and you stand there and allow it. I have to guard my heart, my mind, and my space. The situation I referenced definitely taught me to ask questions, advocate for myself, and learn the culture in which I work.

As we know, sometimes you have to do what you need to do to get what you need to get. I applied for unemployment and anyone knows that if you resign from an employer most times you do not get unemployment. It can be contested. Fortunately, it was not contested and I received unemployment for 26 weeks which bought me enough time to ensure my bills were paid, work on my next strategy which was to find another job and re-enroll in school. I was back to temping again. This was the most humbling experience for me.

I started temping at an agency doing mail merges and stuffing envelopes while two peers from high school had recently graduated from college and were employed full-time with benefits at the same company. This was a reality check for me. I started comparing my situation to theirs. We had graduated high school together so we would have completed our four years of college at the same university together. I was still a bit angry, sad, disappointed and was thinking about what I could and should have done differently. How does this relate to grace and grit?

I had to push my pride to the side and walk into that office every day to work and get a paycheck. I was hurt. I would beat myself up daily for a month or so wondering how I could be so naïve and just sign a letter. But now it was about survival. That was the fire and inspiration I needed to see. I showed up at that temporary agency and gave my all. I learned different software programs and how to mail merge and was the most efficient envelope stuffer there...at least in their eyes. For me, I knew once the work was completed, the job assignment would be over and I could move on to something else. So I was there early and stayed late to complete the project. My time was up. The temporary job placement agency saw my work ethics and fast-paced style and sent me to another assignment. This was my bread and butter to live and take care of my daughter. I was simultaneously looking for permanent, full-time work while networking with people I knew had jobs in various corporations. I received a phone call from a coworker I met while on a temporary assignment. She advised me the company was hiring and encouraged me to apply.

I applied and was called for a job interview. The coworker gave me advice on the department and buzzwords to use during the interview. I knew nothing about the legal field so I was trying to remember everything she shared with me in addition to the information I had researched. My hair was done and nails were nicely manicured. I had on a navy blue dress with pearls and I wore it with confidence in spite of being extremely nervous. I got to the interview and the questions were coming left and right. I was fumbling with my words and everything I had memorized escaped me. Needless to say, I bombed the interview. I left revisiting my responses and trying (in my head) to somehow make it right and make sense of my answers. In my heart, I knew that being called back for a second interview was less than slim to none.

In a few weeks, I received a phone call from the human resources department, advising me that they had filled the position in the litigation department, but another position had opened up for second shift and I would work as a floater. I calmly agreed but when I hung up the phone, I was screaming and thanking God for the opportunity. A floater position would allow me to learn the work of all departments, so I did not need to know the terms, duties and responsibilities starting in the position.

I was offered second shift work which worked in my favor. During the day, I was able to volunteer and be involved in my daughter's education and when I went to work, my mom and aunt were available to care for her. I felt as if this was a win-win for me. To top it off, I was full time, had benefits and was making significantly more than what I was paid with the staffing agency, the previous job I had that resulted in a forced resignation and even what I anticipated.

This was the start of something great. Grace was extended to me and Grit gave me the courage to stay focused hoping to land something soon even though obstacles were in my way. Of course, I had those days and moments when I questioned the process but each day I would get up and go into the world with expectation, hoping and praying that a change would come. Had I given up, I would not have been interviewed, seeking better or even wanting to do better. I may have been in pity party mode looking for someone to either host a party or join me in mine.

There will be times that even when you cannot see the light or have an understanding of what is actually going on, that you must deliberately continue down the path you set for yourself. One step at a time…hoping and knowing that it will all work out for your good. There is light that will shine through even in dark situations. *Look for the light!*

TURN YOUR FACE
TOWARDS THE SUN,
LET THE SHADOWS FALL
BEHIND YOU.

~MAORI PROVERB

F.A.I.L. FORWARD

If you fail, never give up because F.A.I.L. means "First Attempt In Learning."
End is not the end. In fact E.N.D. means "Effort Never Dies". If you get
NO as an answer, remember that N.O. means "Next Opportunity!

The word FAIL or FAILURE is used or viewed in a negative context. If someone is admitting to failing at something, I doubt they would be extremely overjoyed and beaming with smiles of happiness. Failure is not something a person readily admits. You might consider it but no one wants to admit they failed at something. Think about a child. If a child gets an A or B on a test, they are happy and may run home to tell his or her parent or guardian. If a child gets an F on a test, I doubt he or she would run home yelling and bragging about it. At least, not from my perspective.

An employee does not brag at the office about how a project failed. An entrepreneur does not highlight all of his or her failed attempts at something. As I mentioned, failure or failing at something has always been viewed as negative even though we might pretend that it is no big deal. This dates back to the beginning of the book when I talked about my uncertainties and different experiences that led to my overthinking of situations and decisions. I was afraid to fail at something. So to play it safe as much as possible, I became extremely over-cautious. I did not want to fail. Boy, have times changed!

When I released my first book, I sold t-shirts, sweatshirts, and coffee mugs that aligned to the theme and framework of my book. One of my coffee mugs was "Failure is Never an Option." Yes it's a cool cliché but for me this was a reminder for me and others who purchased the mug that *failing* was never an option. Here's why…

The word FAIL simply means First Attempt In Learning. I wouldn't dare go around bragging about all my many failed attempts but what I do know is that everything I do or desire to do has a learning element to it. If it is something I am new at, then I need to learn it from scratch. It could be something I am a bit more experienced with. Nonetheless, it is still learning as things and people change. I had to consciously program my mind to know that it was okay if I did not succeed at something. I am great but I cannot be great at everything (*insert smiley face here*).

That would be considered perfection and there's no such thing. If I attempted to do something and did the best that I could possibly do, then I did not fail. I did the best that I could and although I may have fallen short, it was my first attempt in learning. I now have the experience and the learned lesson from that experience to now use toward betterment. I could take the new learned information and try it again or I could take the information and try something brand new altogether. If you learn from it then I don't see fail or failure in it. It's when we have that "give up" mentality that we fail. We surrender our ideas, we lose excitement and energy, and we no longer believe in ourselves, our abilities and capabilities. We, in turn, become defeated mentally and emotionally. That, in my opinion, is failure.

Should you ever get to this point when you feel like giving up, here are a few strategies that worked for me and continue to be my blueprint:

- **Develop an "I won't quit" and "I can and I will" attitude**. Make a promise to yourself to see it through. Whatever that "it" is at the time, make up in your mind that you won't quit. Pray, get focused, give it your all, and do the best that you can possibly do. When you are giving something your all and it doesn't work out then you can walk away with your confidence in tact because you did not give up or give in. You stayed the course!

- **Listen to podcasts or watch videos for inspiration**. Watching or hearing someone else persevere through something inspires and motivates me to keep pushing forward. You can listen to podcasts, watch videos or even get inspiration from others right in your own community.

- **Re-evaluate your "why"**. When I attempt to do something...anything, I first start with "why". Why do I want to do it? If I don't have a "why" then it may be pointless for me to continue because my reason is unclear. Knowing your "why" will keep you motivated when you feel like giving up. Knowing your "why" will give you the energy and fervor to stay the course when you feel like turning back around. Knowing your "why" keeps you grounded. If I am at a place of giving up, I need to re-evaluate my "why". My "why" is similar to gas in a car. It will keep me going. When I run out of "why" then it's a strong possibility the motivation will dwindle and run out as well.

- **Use a different strategy**. You could be hitting a roadblock because you keep doing the same thing which produces the same results. If what you are currently doing doesn't seem to be working or yielding the results you intended, then you must (1) assess your current situation and strategy, (2) use any and all information that you have acquired, and (3) try a different approach. If there is a will then find a way.

- **Invest in yourself**. As we give of our time and money to causes that are near and dear to our heart and support people and businesses near and far, use the same time and money to invest in yourself. I have seen this quote appear in many places lately specifically tied to self-care, "You cannot give or pour from an empty cup." In my opinion, that quote applies to every area of my life: financial, spiritual, emotional, professional, and mental.

For me, I have always had a seemingly endless to-do list. Just when I think I am completing a few things and crossing them off the list, other tasks are added. I wear many hats: wife, mother, director, adjunct lecturer, entrepreneur, philanthropist, speaker, author...and the list goes on. Each role requires different tasks. In a few instances, some of the tasks might overlap. However, for the most part, they are separate and apart. This requires me to prioritize my work. When you love what you do you can get lost in the work and lose track of time and people.

I consider what has to be done today and even right now and what can wait. This is how I plan everything. People tell me often, "You do so much" or they say "I don't know how you do it. Where do you get the energy?" I prioritize! I prioritize the *urgent*, the *now*, the *then*, the *this can wait* and dismiss the *won't happens*. For example, if I have sole responsibility of a project and it is not a collaborative effort then I complete it in chunks. Meaning, I list all the work that is required for that particular project and then I prioritize the tasks of what needs to happen now or prior to the next step occurring in order to stay on task. If it's a collaborative project, then I assure all those involved have a complete understanding of expectations and the tasks are assigned as needed.

Priorities can sometimes shift. When I feel myself getting distracted, I make a conscious effort to re-examine, re-address and reroute the plan. Let's get back to the quote... "You cannot give or pour from an empty cup." Again, I am more conscious of what I am doing now than I was years ago. If I don't feel like doing something then I don't. If I need to re-address my priorities and shift things around then I do. If I don't feel like going somewhere, I don't. If I need to say "no" to someone or something, I do. For the record, my "no's" are not mean or rude. They are said with all politeness. I am sure it is not what the receiver may want to hear but I know my boundaries and limitations. I would rather give my all with a spirit of excellence than to do something half-assed (pardon the language). That would be a disservice to myself and others. I know it is not always as simple as I have stated but it is so important to remember how you invest your time and energy.

If you want to take a class, take it. If you want to learn a different skill, then take the time and learn it. If you wish to take a vacation, then plan it. If you want another job, polish your resume and start looking. If you want to start a business, then first think about what you want to do and then try it. If you want to start exercising, then look for things to motivate you: read, get a gym buddy, or join a Facebook group for health and wellness. I know life gets in the way and things may come at you from all different angles. While you have much to give to this universe, never neglect yourself in the process. Invest in yourself and remember you cannot pour or give from an empty cup. *Keep refilling as often as you must.*

TIRED OF STARTING OVER? STOP GIVING UP.

~MARK GOSINGTIAN

DON'T GIVE UP!

Giving up doesn't always mean you are weak;
sometimes it means you are strong enough to let go.

.

An opportunity presented itself for me to speak to a group of teens who were considered "at-risk." This was out of the norm for me because most of my speaking engagements and events were geared toward young adults (20+ and up). I remember a few nights before, I was praying and asking God for direction and the words to to keep their attention and inspire them to think differently. This was an audience I had never addressed. Whenever I tried to come up with an outline I would find myself doodling on the paper and being sidetracked by other things. However, I never stressed about it because I felt a sense of peace with thinking that God had me.

The morning of the speech, I called my younger cousin MiMi and we talked about it a few minutes. I asked her if she was in the situation of the teens what would she want to hear? She gave me a few pointers as to what she would want to hear and have heard. I asked her if anyone she had heard before inspired her to think differently? She then proceeded to tell me that when she has a rough day she would think back to one of the "talks" and would get a bit of strength in knowing that some people may have greater challenges than her and she just tries to press through the feelings and situation. In her exact words she told me, "Tam, I see you as a role model now. People don't know some of the challenges you faced unless you tell them. They see the smiles and your grind but they don't know where you came from and the struggle. Be real with them. Let them know who you are. When people see who you are, they can relate better to you because they hear the "person" and not some fake made up shit."

She knew how I felt all my life. I can't pretend to be someone I am not. In different environments I may have to switch it up every now and then but when it comes to being me and keeping it real, that's all I know how to do. Just to clarify, when I said switch it up I am saying there is a time and place for everything. When I am at work, I conduct myself differently than when I am at home, at church, at the gym, etc. Some people might call it code switching. I call it adapting to my surroundings.

So, I stopped and grabbed a cup of coffee, said a prayer and drove to speak to the teens. I had three poster size pictures. One was a picture of me now. The business professional with a crisp blue suit and makeup. I advised them about my career as an author, director, and adjunct lecturer and explained the roles and responsibilities of each. Then I picked up the poster picture of me as a youth with various pictures around it: a picture of my father, a picture of me when I had my first daughter, a picture of me with my younger brother who was always glued to my hip, a picture of me in high school, and a picture of me hanging out. I talked through each picture to explain what was going on with me and in and around me at that time. That's when their ears perked and their eyes widened.

Once I finished with that picture, I picked up the last poster board which was a picture of my "hood" that represented drug infestation, crime, bars on windows, and breezeways. One young male was like, "Miss, you were in the trenches." I had no clue what that meant so I asked for an explanation. Trenches meant "hood" aka "ghetto" to them.

That picture meant struggle, poverty, and community to me. This was a place where I felt safe even though there was violence. Everyone knew each other and was struggling to make ends meet and stay alive. And so I did a similar speech with the same three posters as five groups rotated in and out of the classroom in 30 minute increments. The last group I had was about 6 young girls. One came in looking extremely angry, one shy, and the rest seemed happy go lucky. I gave them the same spiel of my story with the posters and closed with, "Does anyone have any questions?"

There was one young girl in the front, the shy looking one, who raised her hand and asked me, "Miss did you ever feel like giving up?" I paused for about three seconds and responded "Absolutely!" There were numerous times that the thought crossed my mind. There was only so much I could say because we were pressed for time but I told her that I did feel like giving up at times. She opened the door and I knew that was my opportunity to speak life to her and anyone else in the room who felt that way. Giving up is easy and each day we have the power of choice.

There is no effort and energy exerted when walking away. You just walk away! The hardest part is trying to press your way through when you don't know what to expect, where you will land and how you even ended up there. The motivation to keep going comes from "something." It can be an intrinsic motivation. That inner drive that pushes you to keep moving forward or it can be extrinsic and found on the outside of you that pushes you to keep moving forward.

In my case, my motivation came from the external realm (around me)....my daughters. Then it seems as I acquired some knowledge and gained more wisdom during my self-reflection and self-discovery phase (after divorce), the motivation and drive stemmed from the innermost part of me. It did not happen overnight.

The session concluded, I had lunch and left. On the drive home, I was thinking about the young girl and the question she asked me. There were many times that I considered giving up. When my mom was struggling with an addiction, I literally wanted to give up because I was angry, rebellious and it was hard for me to understand how she could choose it over me and my brother. In my head, I felt like she was choosing it over us but in all reality drugs had a hold on her at the time and she really wasn't in the right frame of mind to even think or consider how we felt.

I thought about giving up while raising my oldest daughter as a single parent. It was hard watching and hearing about her father coming and going as he pleased with no care in the world and no regard for her or even me. At this time, giving up would have been me not sacrificing by working and going to school while raising her. I could have given up hope and just settled with life the way that it was. I could have given up on my dreams and settled for mediocrity. That would have been my version of giving up. Basically, forgetting about pursuing things that could potentially make me and us better because the struggle was too hard and the future appeared dim.

I thought about giving up after my divorce and back to being a single parent. I had to start all over again which wasn't easy: work, church, the schools my daughters attended, where we lived, etc. I was not only fighting for rights in court but I was fighting for my character, integrity, dignity and peace of mind. Giving up would have been forsaking my happiness and tolerating a situation that robbed me of my peace. There are many variations of how and when people "give up." Everyone has the power of choice. We can choose to do good or bad. We can choose to be happy or sad. We can choose to get up or lay down. We can choose to save or spend. We can choose to eat or starve. You get the gist of it. We can choose to give up or persevere. I can't help but wonder what made her ask me that question.

I did a quick exercise and asked each person to write down on paper what they wanted in life as far as a career goal. I then had them list 3 to 4 things they could do daily that would lead them to that goal. I told them that every day they wake up and open their eyes, they have a choice to make and they should ask themselves, "What can I do today that will bring me closer to my goal by tomorrow?" As I closed, I asked each of them what they had gotten out of our time together. One youth said, "think before I act." Another youth said, "Where you start doesn't have to be where you finish." Another youth said, "Everyone started from somewhere and no one is perfect." The shy girl who asked the question if I ever considered giving up blurted out, "Don't give up!"

I wanted to literally hug her but I kept my composure and told them all how special they were. Had I given up, I would not have been there with them. If they give up, then they can't meet others who are waiting for them in their future. This really blessed my soul.

We all go through things. I can't say I have experienced extremely bad things. I've had some challenging times and I know some may have had it better than me and some perhaps even worse. But I don't compare my situation to anyone else's because my journey is mine and their journey is theirs. Instead of comparing and trying to "measure" up to the image, perception, and expectations of others, we must strive daily at being the best version of ourselves. Know that obstacles, challenges, and triumphs produce strength, ambition and GRIT! Everything that has happened...happened! What are we going to do now is the question.

ONE OF THE HARDEST
THINGS IN LIFE IS
DECIDING WHETHER YOU
SHOULD GIVE UP OR
TRY HARDER.

~PICTUREQUOTES.COM

USE YOUR TIME WISELY

Time waits for no one.

Every single person in this world gets the same 365 days a year, 52 weeks in a year, 7 days in one week, 24 hours in a day, 60 minutes in each hour, and 60 seconds in a minute. What we choose to do with our time each and every day is totally up to each one of us. We have choices. We can waste the time or we can be productive and maximize every moment and opportunity.

Whether we are having fun, stressing out about something or dealing with a particular situation, time will keep ticking. Have you ever had so much fun that you wish you could stay in that moment a little longer? Have you ever gone on vacation or experienced something surreal that you wish you could pause time and bask in it a little longer? Have you ever been stressed about a situation and couldn't wait for the time to come and go? And guess what, whether it was good or bad, time came and time passed.

Those moments were temporary. This life is temporary. Things can and will change in the blink of an eye. This is why it is so important to stay present, live in the right now, create memories, and just live. When we look back, the time just keeps on ticking and we have no way of stopping it.

A good friend of mine was preparing for an interview. She was all worked up about it. This is normal. It happens to me too. But this particular time, I was able to see nerves and emotions at work because I was on the outside helping her to get refocused. I asked her if she was prepared and felt ready and she said yes. We went over a few typical and standard questions and she knocked them out the park. I asked her why she was so nervous and she said her interview was within the next hour. I asked her to take a deep breath and then proceeded with this....

"You have nothing to worry about. What God has for you, is for you. You have prepared as best as you could. Your nerves and emotions are getting the best of you because time is ticking and the time is near. The interview is in one hour and by the next hour and forty-five minutes, the interview will be behind you. You may think about ways you could have answered the questions differently or you may feel confident in all your responses. When the time is up, the time is up. From the interview, you will be waiting to get a phone call or letter to advise you of the status or next step. This will happen all in due TIME! Will you continue to stress yourself out and make yourself sick or will you allow TIME to take its course? Before you know it, it will all be said and done one way or another and this time will have passed."

I've learned to take my own advice. I get jitters too and if I don't check them, my nerves will get the best of me. I have to remind myself that "this too shall pass." Nothing ever remains the same. Life will have its ups and downs, its peaks and valleys. We must develop coping skills so that when the downs come, we can dig deep to reflect on grace and grit to be determined that the current situation will not remain the same. We cannot sit back and expect it to change; we must work and exercise our faith to bring about change.

We must stay present so when the highs abound, we can humbly appreciate the moment by living in the NOW, soaking it all in, and staying present. Never look down on someone else unless you are extending a hand to help them up. Do know that time will pass and the tide can change. And I must stress this as well, try your best not to burn bridges. You just never know when you might need that very same person. I said all that not to have you uptight but more so to bring awareness to the fact that EVERYTHING is temporary, time is constant and death is something we cannot escape.

Who and what gets the majority of your time?

Are you content or are you happy? (there is a difference)?

What can you do differently with your time that will bring you HAPPINESS?

Examine the people you are connected to. Do they bring stress or peace?

The previous questions should get you thinking about your current state if you have not done so already. Think about how valuable your time is, how you spend it and who you spend it with. Think about connections in your personal and professional environment. Is there anything you wish to change?

Change is hard and it may not happen overnight. Consider and ask yourself this question....how do I wish to spend my time? Time will keep ticking whether we want it to or not. The beginning (birth) and the end (death) are certain. What we do in between that time (the dash) is totally up to us.

In memory of my aunt, the late and great, Mamie "Peanut" Johnson, 1935 – 2017. *Google her name!*

"Time only moves forward, you don't get it back."
Tyesha W.

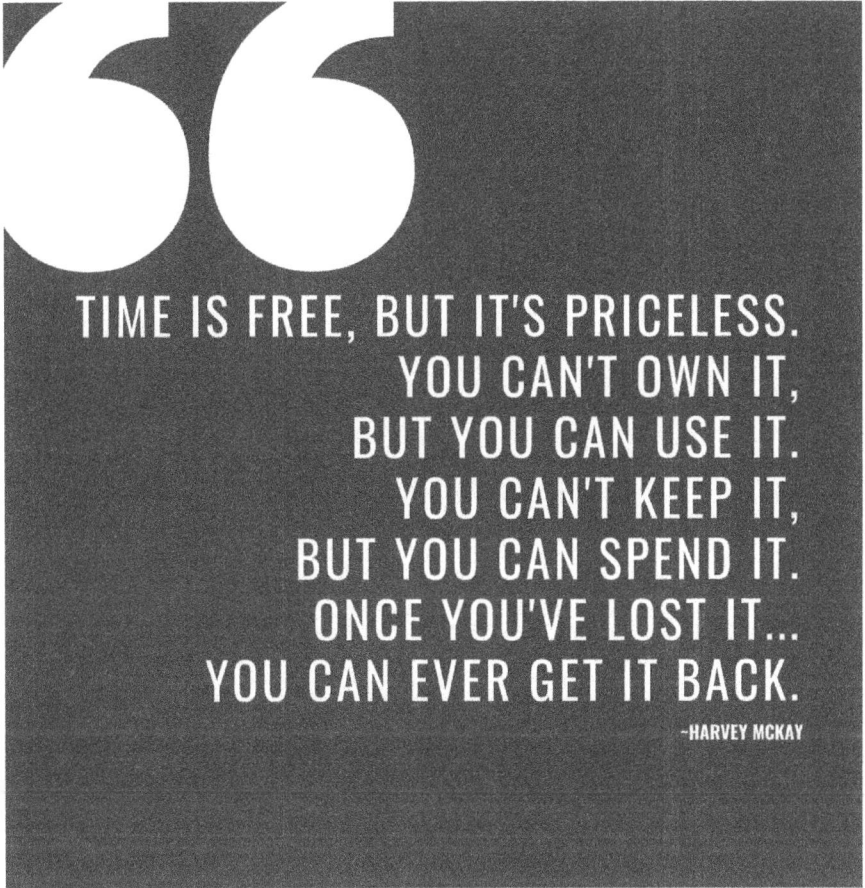

TIME IS FREE, BUT IT'S PRICELESS.
YOU CAN'T OWN IT,
BUT YOU CAN USE IT.
YOU CAN'T KEEP IT,
BUT YOU CAN SPEND IT.
ONCE YOU'VE LOST IT...
YOU CAN EVER GET IT BACK.

-HARVEY MCKAY

STAY READY!

When opportunity knocks will you be ready to answer?

I never want to be in a position where an opportunity is presented to me but I am not prepared or ready for it. The first thing I do is understand myself and my interests. Then I prepare for it. Preparing for an opportunity means I would research information, read and develop my knowledge and skills in that area. I may not know EVERYTHING or be an EXPERT but I equip myself with at least the bare minimum information and build from there.

My best way of learning has always been through a hands-on approach. I have to be in it to see how it works and how it is connected. For example, I have worked for a company where I was promoted to various departments and earned different titles within each capacity. I first had to learn the culture. Whenever you start a new job or new role, there is learning that comes with it. In addition to culture, you may need to know and learn a new piece of technology. You may just need to learn and understand how your role and the work fit within the larger scope of the organization. I had the required credentials to get me to the interview table. My foundation was knowing and understanding the organization: the mission, vision, core values, and who we served as well as my previous, hands on experience that allowed me to develop specific technical and transferable skills. This was my baseline. To build upon that, I would take the time to read and research as much information as possible such as key words being used in meetings, analyzing data, asking questions, and remaining teachable. In addition, I would seek additional professional development opportunities, work on focus groups, intentionally connect with other people who are doing similar work, and volunteer to be a part of or lead projects. Most importantly, I remained teachable. We should always have a teachable spirit and mindset and be like a sponge to soak in all the knowledge we can get our hands on.

Now suppose I did not have a degree; that alone may have disqualified me from the race. Sometimes it's not what you know, it's who you know but let's just assume that I knew no one and everything was strictly based on skills and qualifications. I wanted to ensure my skills were sharp and my qualifications were evident.

When I first obtained my degree, I was seeking employment and was told on a few occasions that I had the degree and not the experience. So how did I build that experience? I volunteered in a similar agency that allowed me to continue to develop my skills in order to list current and relevant experience on my resume. There is no quick solution. It is all on a case-by-case basis. I just wanted to provide an example of how I invested in myself just in case an opportunity was presented so that I could be ready. And, this isn't to say that it's a one size fits all. People will choose who they "feel" would be a good fit for the job. I have received quite a few "no's" in my lifetime thus far.

However, I continually invest in myself by learning and learning some more. Whether it is professional or personal, I do believe in self-development. Self-development increased my confidence and self-esteem. I can learn anything I want if I choose to. That is my mindset. If I want to know anything I can read, learn and apply what I've learned. And with the internet, learning is at our fingertips;

information flows right into our homes. We no longer have to go to a library if we choose not to.

When you stop learning, you stop growing. There is more knowledge available today than there was when I was a child. It is our responsibility to understand and develop the gift that God has placed in each one of us.

I've always wanted to write a book. Remember, I mentioned before that I had no clue about writing and publishing a book of my own. How did I learn?

- I started writing.

- I went to the library and flipped through different genres of books to understand the format.

- I researched and googled how to write a book and read through suggested articles.

- I talked to authors I knew to get advice and they would always advise me to just *START WRITING*!

It took me some time to get through numbers 2 and 3. There is a wealth of information out there. Through my research, the common theme I kept reading about was to establish my writing space and just write. I had the ideas in my head so I just needed to put them on paper.

Once I started writing, fear, procrastination, and the struggles of life kicked in and that's why I had my stop and start moments over and over again.

But guess what now? Because I remained teachable and took the time to do my initial research and pursue my dream, I was able to stay on the path of development by expanding my network, learning new tools of technology, and understanding and reflecting on how I first started.

This is my second time around and although some things seem a bit more common for me now, it is still a learning process. Never be afraid or ashamed to learn. Continue to build on your knowledge base in order to be and stay ready!

> WHEN OPPORTUNITY
> KNOCKS, DON'T LET FEAR
> HOLD YOU BACK.
> OPEN THE DOOR AND
> EMBRACE THE OPPORTUNITY
> THAT HAS COME FORTH.
>
> ~ABUNDANCETAPESTRY.COM

DEFINE YOUR OWN SUCCESS

There is no elevator to success. You have to take the stairs.

Success can be defined in many ways. In fact, I took a poll of what success means to others and here are some of the responses I received:

Success means goals being achieved after releasing fear (Jessica H.)

Success means completion. No matter how many times I fail, success is getting back up until I finish the goal (Joan T.)

Success is living life on my own terms and doing the things that maximize my potential and brings me joy (Johnnie I.)

Success is conquering my fears
(Jenn O.)

Success is accomplishment in any shape or form
(Dee H.)

Success has many interpretations and is defined by the individual in his or her pursuit for success.

We run after so many things in pursuit of success: careers, relationships, money, validation, education, and status, to name a few. What does success mean to you? I ask you this in all sincerity. We must understand and define success on our own terms and not the terms of others.

Otherwise, we may find ourselves in pursuit of this falsehood of what success is supposed to be because we allowed it to be defined by others based upon what they may have imposed on us or what we have seen to be success for them.

Success is not what someone else wants for you but what you want and desire for yourself. As you can see from the definitions shared from others, if we are not sure, we can easily fall into someone else's definition of what success is or can be.

I've had someone tell me how successful I am. I stood there like a deer caught in the headlights. I was curious to know why they thought I was "successful" so I asked. They told me I was successful because I had a good job, beautiful children, I was active in my community, had just written and released a book and I had a great marriage. To this person, this all appeared as a sign of success. What they may or may not know is that this was my second marriage which means my first one ended in divorce. If it was successful, then I would still be married to my first husband. Although my children are beautiful and smart, my youngest has a health challenge that can be quite difficult to manage at times. Even though my career is fulfilling, each year most employees are left wondering if they will have a job because of the financial constraints in the city. As with any relationship, my husband and I have our ups and downs. There are times when we pluck each other's last nerves and there are times when we don't want to be away from each other at all. I said all this to say, it all APPEARED to be a success because a person can only see or know so much unless they are in it to see or hear it firsthand. It is all perception looking from the outside in.

I am most grateful for my husband, children, career, and the opportunity to give back in my community and venture into entrepreneurship. I am humbled by the opportunities that have been provided to me. I also know that I worked my ass off and it did not come easy. I had to prepare and work for them and constantly prove myself. I had to face my fears and talk myself through just about everything I have done.

I know that things could always be worse so I try not to focus and stay glued on the negative. I keep optimism in the forefront and positivity around me as much as possible. Have you ever experienced a "bad" morning when nothing seems to be going right? Maybe you haven't, but I have. I realize the more I focus on how bad of a day it is, the more the universe delivers what I am expecting to happen. I usually tell myself when having a bad morning that it can only get better. Purposely, I look for that better in order to change my mindset and shift my mood. The same is true for success. I have purposely persevered in pursuit of achieving my goals and have accomplished things I have set out to do in pursuit of success. However, my accomplishments are elements of that success. Although I have achieved certain areas and levels of success, I always push harder striving to be a better me. What I have learned to do is to not be so laser focused on the big goals that I forget to celebrate the small wins while enroute to success. NOW I make a more conscious effort to celebrate the small AND the big, the great AND the not so great with the intention to learn about myself along the way while building on the successes and wins that will carry me to the next phase.

Overall, I want to be happy. Who doesn't? But being happy is a state of being. Regardless of whether one is successful or not, he or she can make a choice to be happy. I don't attribute success to happiness. If I said success to me is being wealthy, I could have the wealth but be miserable. This is why I don't attribute this kind of success to happiness. In order to define success for yourself, you first need to know and understand what matters to you, who you are, and what you want to achieve in life. Otherwise, you end up living up to someone else's definition of success and allowing perception to become the reality.

People see you as "successful" if you are where they are trying to go. They may not consider what it took to get there and they won't know unless they ask. I know for me in general it came with a lot of learning, sacrificing, and a whole lot of patience. In the world of entrepreneurship, I have quickly learned in a short time that it takes a lot of hustle and grind. It did not come easy but it is so worth it. Success to me is getting all my ideas out of my head and into practice. I haven't arrived but I am well on my way. I am taking more risks, conquering my fears and stepping outside of my comfort zone. This is my daily reminder of success. I am further along than when I first started and that in and of itself is SUCCESS to me as I strive for progress and not perfection!

SUCCESS IN LIFE COMES
WHEN YOU SIMPLY REFUSE
TO GIVE UP, WITH GOALS SO
STRONG THAT OBSTACLES,
FAILURE, AND LOSS ONLY
ACT AS MOTIVATION.

~DREAMSQUOTE.COM

CATCH THE CURVE BALLS

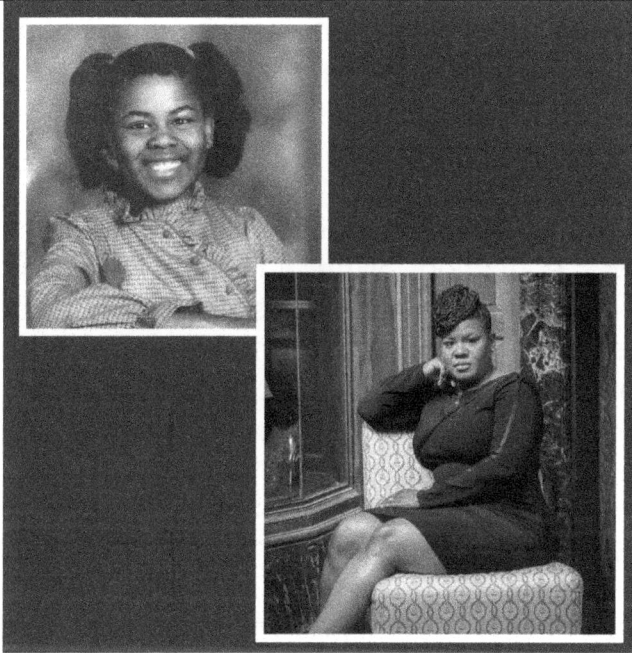

As a child, no one aspires to be an addict, alcoholic, victim of any kind, worthless, homeless, broke, or convicted felon, to name a few. When you ask a first or second grader what they want to be when they grow up, the response is usually a doctor, nurse, lawyer, teacher, social worker, professional sports player or artist. We have dreams as a young child but as we grow up, life happens.

Think back to when you were a child. What did you want to be when you grew up? What are you now? Is it the path you intended or were there dips and turns along the way?

As a child I wanted to be a teacher. You would find me playing school with my friends and cousins. I was the one playing the "teacher" role, creating assignments, giving out homework, making ditto sheets and prepping for class, especially during the summer when we had an entire day of free time. At night, I would use blank sheets of paper and make words out of dots so the assignment would be to trace the words. I would make up math problems such as 1+7 = __. And, of course, I would correct the papers with a red pen. I was playing the role of what I saw as a teacher.

When I enrolled into college right after high school, my major was education. When I became aware that I would have to student teach and have someone evaluate me while in a classroom, I became extremely fearful of that because I did not enjoy speaking in front of people. I then changed my major to Liberal Arts. Needless to say, due to other circumstances and misunderstandings, I did not finish college while I was there at that time. I share some of the reasons why I did not finish in the book #GoalGetter.

After working and having my daughter, I enrolled in a local community college with a major in Liberal Arts. I still was not at a place of being able to overcome that fear of public speaking. After graduating with my Associates degree, I went on to earn my Bachelors and Masters degrees while working and raising my daughter. I still had the love for teaching and the fear of public speaking. The opportunity presented itself for me to be a part of a yearlong fellowship program specifically within the community college system. I applied and was accepted. I was paired with an amazing business professor and mentor, Heidi.

During my fellowship, I had the opportunity to teach in a college setting, create lesson plans, and participate in professional learning offered by the fellowship

82

program to develop my skills and build confidence while learning as I went along. Once the fellowship program concluded, I was offered an adjunct position with the community college system and am presently still affiliated with the college as a business professor.

This story goes back to the previous chapter titled "Stay Ready." The opportunity, though I thought I had missed it, presented itself and I was prepared. Each and every day, I had to talk myself through it. I had a dream as a child and I believe God connected the dots for me. I had no clue what I was doing and how I was going to get there but I just kept walking, believing that I could. I am most grateful for the opportunities that have been presented and offered to me. Even though I felt that I could not do it, I wanted it so bad that I had to live outside of my fear.

As you can see, some decisions are within our own control and then some are totally out of our control. Some situations we found ourselves in as adults were due to decisions we made and some were made for us due to those we associated with. If this journey or path to your right now was straight and narrow, then you have certainly beat the odds and stayed true to your dreams and aspirations. If by chance, you have faced challenges along the way and fell off course, then you are no different than millions of other people in this world and that includes ME.

I intentionally titled this chapter "Curve Ball" for a reason. When I hear the term curve ball, I automatically think about (1) the game of baseball, and (2) the idea that the pitcher who threw the curve ball is expecting the ball to shift or curve as it travels to the batter. It is purposeful and is not intended to travel in a straight line. So now, how does this apply to your life?

As a child you may have anticipated being a certain way, obtaining a certain career, being in a certain relationship, and having a different life than what you may be currently experiencing. To me, this is the curve ball.

All the setbacks that came with my first divorce was my curve ball. But they say, "A setback is a setup for a comeback." I was on a mission to come back from a dark place where my character was assassinated. My daughters had to change schools. We moved to a different town. Our church and church family changed. I even had to find a new job. I was angry, hurt and frustrated. I was drowning. I had two choices: sink or swim.

From childhood into adulthood, I have experienced plans that were deferred and deterred. Relationships ended. Jobs started and ended. Careers shifted. Somehow the train derailed after one helluva bumpy ride. So now what do you do?? You plan forward! You take **EVERYTHING**, the good and the bad that you have experienced, learned, went through, overcame, struggled with, adjusted to, dealt with, cried through and pushed passed and you make it work for YOU. Whether you are an author, entrepreneur, spouse, parent, in recovery, divorced, or just starting out *everything* you have encountered so far is a wealth of information that you can use to your benefit.

If you struggled with something, you know now what not to do and even how to do it differently and better. If you failed at some things then you know now what to do the next time and again, what not to do. Besides, there is no such thing as failure as long as you are trying and learning from the mistakes made. You are unique, and it is my opinion and belief that each and every person in this world has a unique gift and talent. Unique meaning being only one of its kind. There is no other person in this world like me or you. God made us just how we are with our own specific DNA and uniqueness. How marvelous is that? I was having a "moment" as I was adding the finishing touches to this book. I had to remind myself how unique I am. I can't expect people to remind me of this or build me up. I have to tell myself how beautiful and wonderful I am. How unique and fly I am. I don't care what has happened in the past or what is currently happening as you read this. Just pause for a second and think about YOURSELF. If you need to look in the mirror and just stand there and admire yourself then do just that. We forget to love on ourselves. Well let me speak for myself. I was so caught up in chasing my dreams and pursuing my passion that I forgot to pause and just bask in the woman I had become. I am not where I want to be but I am certainly not where I used to be. I didn't give myself enough credit for the hard work I had already put in and continue to put in even as I type. If I don't love on me, encourage myself, and build me up then who will?

I am sure you have heard, "When life gives you lemons, make lemonade." It's the same concept with curveballs. When you are up to bat, you have the opportunity to hit that curve ball clean out of the park. As you stand on the home plate trying to figure things out or perhaps you are well along the way, know that curve balls will most times be a part of the process. Batter up! Don't wait for a soul to help you. *Go hard and make it happen for yourself!*

START LIVING; STOP EXISTING

Speak What You Seek Until You See What You've Said

I was heading out to work one morning and as I was driving, I had no music on but got lost in my thoughts. I was thinking back over my life: friends, career choices, family members and just different situations and circumstances. Without giving much thought to the direction I was going, I ended up on the street of my job. I mean I had literally driven to work through street lights, highways, some rights and left turns but ended up at my destination. My route was so routine that I knew where I was going even if I didn't give much thought to my sense of direction. When I realized this, I pulled over on the street across from my parking garage and just sat there people watching for about 30 minutes.

Again, I got lost in my thoughts and tears welled up in my eyes as I reflected on *Life*. I reflected on my past marriage, my current marriage, my children being born and raised thus far, and decisions I neglected to make because I was afraid to do so. I thought about family members and friends who have passed away and wondered if they felt they had lived their best life or if they passed away with dreams buried inside. Were their dreams unfulfilled? Were there things they wanted to do but put on the back burner thinking they had time later in life to do it? Were they waiting for the "perfect" time or the "perfect" mate?

I watched the trees blow in the wind. I watched the birds fly around. I watched people cross the street and cars stop and go. Immediately, it hit me. We get so caught up in the hustle and bustle of life that we start existing and forget about living. We don't take the time to explore things that bring us pleasure because we are consumed with other things. Our life becomes so routine that we become robots. We wake up, maybe exercise, head off to work, put in 8-10 hour days, get off work, pick up the children, come home, cook, text a few people, pay bills, shower, have sex, go to bed, wake up and repeat. The order may be slightly off depending on the age of our children or relationship status but 3 to 4 of what I have listed above are at least applicable to what each day might look like for us.

I may have taken a vacation here and there but was I living…was my question. I was existing. After my divorce, I was so focused on building myself back up mentally, emotionally, physically, and financially that I was doing everything in my power to survive not live. It's like I woke up one morning and my youngest was a pre-teen and my oldest was a young adult. I was physically there to watch them grow but there were certain things about their upbringing I had forgotten. I realized my joy was gone. My dreams were on the back burner. My priorities were my children as they should have been but I was lost and trying to find my way. I was caught up in people pleasing.

I wanted to be loved and accepted by everyone. I wanted this perfect family that I did not have. I wanted to start and build traditions that would be passed down from one generation to another. I wanted so much more than what I had. I was focused and consumed with it all and everyone else that I forgot about me. If someone asked me at the time, what I enjoyed doing, I would respond with the typical answers such as going on vacation, reading, listening to music, etc. I had to even think about those responses. Did I really enjoy those things or was that the safest response for me because I really did not know what I enjoyed doing? As I sat there in the car crying about the time I had missed, I realized that I did not and could not afford to continue in the same manner. I wanted to be present for my children. I wanted to be present in my marriage. I wanted to live and not exist. So I made a conscious effort to start on this journey of exploration to figure out what really makes me happy, brings me joy and allows me to live as authentically as possible. This is how it all started for me and the advice I would give:

- **Be mindful of your time.** As I stated in a previous chapter, time waits for no one and is very important. How I spent my time was totally up to me. I could spend it waddling in my sorrows, complaining, living in regret and entertaining pointless pity parties or I could use it to build, grow and uplift. I made a decision to use my time wisely with things that were important to ME. This is not to say that I did not tend to things that were of importance to others. However, my time was unbalanced. I would usually spend 60% on others and 40% on me. I had to find balance (50/50) or for the most part increase the percentage and amount of time on my end that was specifically dedicated and focused on ME and modify the percentage spent on the other end.

- **Say NO and be okay with it.** I would feel uneasy if I had to tell someone "no." If someone asked me to do something, whether I wanted to or not, I would try to come through. I was a people pleaser. I became so liberated when I found the word NO in my vocabulary. And guess what, I did not have to explain why I said NO. When I was a child and my mom would tell me no, I would ask why. Her response would be, "*because I said so.*" I should have learned from then that I owed no one an explanation when I said no regardless of how guilty I felt or how they made me feel for saying no. If you don't want to do something then you should not feel forced, awkward or bad about it. I had my reasons for saying No and I had to stick to it. Otherwise, I would do it then regret that I did.

Have you ever done something you really didn't want to do but did it instead? How did it make you feel? Were you happy at first? I know I wasn't. I would do it but then be upset that I did. My energy would change. My attitude might be jacked up and my facial expressions may have shifted. It wasn't the receiver's fault that I was all jacked up. It was my own. I did it. I brought it on myself. I had to ask myself, why do something if you really don't want to do it? Why do it if you will be uneasy and all upset and uptight? I wanted to make the other person happy more than I did myself. The game had to change.

- **Pursue things that are important to you.** Once I discovered what brought joy to my life and made me happy then I had to pursue those things. For so long, I put other people's happiness before my own. Again, leaving me unbalanced and unfulfilled. I had to get a little selfish. People will suck the life out of you if you let them. I was at a place where I refused to continue in that manner. I had to prioritize my life, understand if there was a value added to my life because of it and get things in order.

• **Stop and smell the roses.** Minimize the mundane busyness. People would say to me all the time, "I don't know how you do it. You are everywhere and you do so much." I personally never felt this way. Yes I am busy but I know when to slow down. I have learned how to compartmentalize my life. When I am at work, I am in work mode. When I am home, I am in home mode. When I am with my friends, I am in friend mode. As I am writing this book, I am in author mode. When I am with my daughters, I am in mommy mode. Granted, some responsibilities you just can't compartmentalize and get a break from. However, this approach has allowed me to stay "present" in certain areas of my life. It did not happen naturally at first but as I began to practice, the easier it became. When writing, I would set a timer and write until my time was up. It may not work for everyone but it was worth a try for me. This approach has allowed me to stay "present" in order to take the time to stop and smell the roses, create memories, start traditions, and enjoy "quality" time with others and even myself.

• **You can't force people to like you. Understand this and stop trying**. For some reason, I thought everyone had to like me. If I gave them no reason not to then they should. That was my thinking. I would question myself wondering if I did or said something wrong. If I engage with you in a positive light then I would expect the same in return. If I support you then you should support me. If I did no harm to you then I would expect for you not to

93

harm me. Boyyyyy did I have it wrong. People will dislike you for no apparent reason at all. It could be someone you associate with. It could be a look you have on your face. It could be your progress. It could be the peace that you have. It could be something they misinterpreted in their own head and instead of taking the time to ask questions or seek understanding they took it and ran with it. Or it could just be YOU…point blank period.

Let me be clear and honest; there are people I choose not to deal with. I made a decision a while ago to avoid toxic, negative, and miserable people at all costs. This does not mean that I dislike them. I just choose not to deal with them on a day-to-day basis. Because that is my truth, I know you can't force people to like you. You can be sweet, loving, giving, and supportive. If they don't like you, giving them a slice of apple pie won't change their mind. They will take the pie, smile in your face and still not like you. Don't expend your energy trying to force them to. It is what it is. There are other things to focus your time and energy on.

I am not saying that you dismiss relationships or disregard people you may have had a disagreement with. That is not what I am saying at all. If the relationship means something to you or the other person then you work through it. You talk things out.   You ask questions, seek understanding, make amends and sometimes disagree to agree. You save what you can and build from there.

On the contrary, I am talking about individuals who you know don't like you but yet any chance you get you are trying to suck up and get them to change their mind. Are you kidding me? If you have done nothing wrong then that's their issue not yours. Pray for them and keep it moving. Hurt people hurt people. At no fault of your own or even mine, you can't force anyone to do anything. Leave them alone and focus on YOU. That goes for males or females. Friend or Foe. When a person shows you who they are....believe them!

- **Be mindful of what you speak**. It is my belief the power of life and death is in the tongue. I have a choice to speak positive over my life and situation or I can speak negative. Whenever something negative comes to mind, I automatically cancel that thought with something positive. My thoughts had to change if I wanted to start living and stop existing. I had to mentally and emotionally change my thoughts and actions. I had to see the glass as half full and not half empty. I had to choose my words wisely. I had to be intentional with what I allowed to consume me and who I associated with. I had two choices. I could worry or pray but I could not do both because one cancels out the other.

- **Get rid of the weight and fly with those who lift you.** I had people in my life who only dealt with me when it was to their benefit. If they needed a favor or wanted someone to dump their problems on, they would only call me for those very reasons. They never called to say hello, to check on my well-being or even encourage me. It was always: Can you do me a favor? Can you help me? Or they would just need an ear to discuss all the negative things going on in their life. I was on the receiving end for quite some time. As I stated previously, I wanted to always come through for those who called upon me so I would listen, help, and let them dump and even cry and pray with them. I was not obligated to do that but

I did because I wanted to support them and felt it was my duty to do so. In my eyes, I had to love them back to wholeness because someone did it for me. But I often found myself alone, suffering with no outlet and eventually recognized the pattern. If you can call me for a favor, you can call me to say hello and ask how I am doing. If you can call me to dump your problems then I should be able to dump mine too. Don't just call when you have a need. I felt used, taken advantage of and burdened. So what was I going to do about it? I could no longer allow people to pull me down, to dump their problems on me and then just leave.

If I spent all my time carrying the weight and burden of other people's problems then I would not have any strength to carry my own. If an issue or problem was presented to me by someone and I assisted them by working through it but then ended up putting in more time and energy into it than the person it directly affected, then that was an even bigger problem for me. That's like someone who says they are looking for a job and you end up doing their resume for them, researching places that are hiring, making phone calls, talking to other people on their behalf and doing all the legwork and they are just sitting back doing nothing or the bare minimum. They need to be working just as hard, if not more.

However, for my own sake, I had to be mindful of the weights that brought me down and look for encouragers in my life. I had to fly with people who lifted me, inspired me, who motivated me, believed in me and who wanted to see me succeed. I had to be mindful of the company I kept. This was all a part of me learning to live and not just simply exist. When I existed I allowed people to talk to me and treat me any old kind of way. When I learned to live, I took ownership of what and who I allowed in my life and I held people accountable for the energy they brought into my space, negative and positive.

Take inventory of relationships you currently have. Is it consumed with weights (things or people that bring you down) or lifts (things or people that encourage and inspire you)? Take responsibility for your own happiness and live.

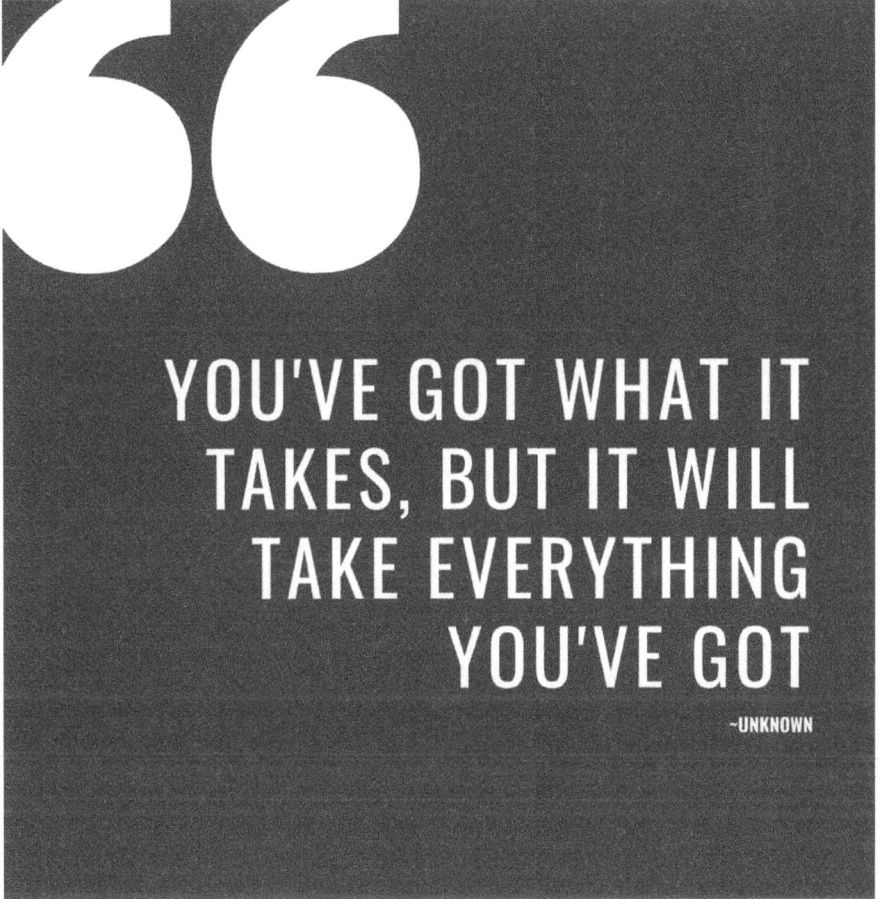

YOU'VE GOT WHAT IT TAKES, BUT IT WILL TAKE EVERYTHING YOU'VE GOT

~UNKNOWN

KEEP YOUR EYES ON THE PRIZE

If the plan doesn't work change the plan but never the goal.

I published a book, met some amazing people, increased my network, added products and additional services to my brand and then I hit a wall. I felt stuck. I had so much I wanted to do and had several ideas of building my next phase of my business. I had people pouring into me what they thought I should be doing and I became sidetracked and overwhelmed.

I had to decide if I wanted to build what I knew to be my own vision or build someone else's vision. Don't get me wrong, I was given good advice but it was not my vision and style of doing things. It was theirs and if I took the advice then I ran the risk of losing my own individuality along with it. This was something I was not willing to do. I did not want to be a copy. I did not want to build a brand that was contrary to what I believed it to be. I did not want to go down the wrong path when I knew this was something that God had already revealed to me.

I had circumstances, closed doors, and even scam artists that tried to take advantage of me being new to this arena of work. In my heart, I knew I was being derailed and I had to take a step back, reflect and re-strategize my plan. When you put in time and effort with something that is near and dear to your heart and you operate in a space that brings you fulfillment, you will get lost in time. There are times when I get so caught up in my work that brings me fulfillment that hours and hours of time will pass and I am flowing in my element. I love this space to be in. It is not draining and overwhelming. It is my peace. Although I am working, I am working from a place of happiness and contentment so it does not even feel like work. It is more pleasure than work.

I usually schedule one to one meetings with someone I call a "thought" partner. When I sit with my thought partner it is a non-judgmental meeting. I share my ideas, thoughts, and plans and my thought partner challenges my thinking that provokes me to consider other ways of doing things or helps me to refine my vision that leads to value creation and alignment of my purpose and passion. For example, I was preparing to speak at a conference. I had an idea of the make-up of the audience but I had several different ways I wanted to approach my subject matter. My ideas were all over the place because I had so much I wanted to share and provide in a short amount of time. I met with my thought partner and he assisted me with mapping out my strategy. Not only did we talk strategy but we talked about dreams, goals, aspirations, and upcoming events. We defined words, talked scriptures, planned forward and we both strategized our next moves. It was a two-way street where we both exchanged valuable information.

So, I got home, prayed, and started preparing for the conference. I had to submit a proposal and when I started writing out the description to submit to the conference host, I just started flowing from a place of creativity that I never knew existed. I was tapping into another area.

I wanted to share my gift but fear prevented me from doing it in the past. I was afraid to speak in public, believe it or not. This conference was a big deal to me. I was able to face my fear and share my story. I was able to meet and connect with other individuals and continue to build my brand. I had to look pass the fear and although I had to pay a speaker fee to participate, I had to invest in myself and step outside of my comfort zone. And even though I had the opportunity to sell my books and merchandise after I presented at the conference with no guarantees to make a profit, the opportunity was priceless for me. I was weighing the pros and the cons and the pros outweighed the cons so I invested and took a chance on myself. I knew what I wanted to do. I had to prepare for it and made up my mind to keep my eyes on the prize.

Everything I was doing NOW was preparing me for my tomorrow. I said ME but in fact it was making a path for everyone and everything connected to me. The information I learn. The paths I take. The hurdles I jump. The obstacles I overcome. It's not just for me to keep to myself. I am building my knowledge base and have been able to share the information with others.

I get people reaching out to me all the time inquiring about specific things or wanting advice. I can only share from my own experience which is why I said it impacts everyone and everything connected to me. I want to see us all win. When you know better you do better. I am learning and growing daily.

"

YOU HAD A PURPOSE BEFORE ANYONE HAD AN OPINION

~TIMOTHY PINA

GET OUT OF YOUR OWN WAY

Often, we are our own worst enemy when working towards our goals.
Robert T. Kiyosaki

We have heard it before. Get out of your own way. Many times we talk ourselves out of decisions before we even attempt to give it a try. Ask me how I know? When I stated in previous chapters that I was an over-thinker and how it took me a long time to make a decision or even take risks, I was telling you the absolute truth. Yes, I was wired this way. I had been this way for a very long time. A few people might have mentioned it to me before but you know when it really hit me? It hit me when my oldest daughter brought it to my attention. I was supposed to teach and show her the way and now she was teaching and showing me. We were in the kitchen talking and sharing. She had just started her business and I was sharing with her a few things I had coming up and how I had it mapped out. I wanted to pick her thoughts and get additional perspectives so I was asking questions. Everything I said, she agreed and said the same thing. I was like .. "No, I want you to tell me what you think." Her response was, "Ma, there is nothing else to say. You covered it all and then some. Everything I was going to suggest you already had it down." And then she asked me, "Why are you so critical of yourself?" All I could do was say, "I know right" and then there was complete silence.

I agreed with her but it hit me like a bulldozer. It was a quick reality check for me. Everything I had done and was doing up to that point, I could find something wrong and think about what I should have done differently. It could be something so miniscule. I did not internalize it to the point where I would be feeling down and out but I did not give myself enough credit for what I had done, was doing and even accomplished. I was in my own way.

Fast forward to right now…I realize that was a habit for me. I was my own worst critic. I wanted to find the mistakes before anyone else could point them out. I wanted to be the best at everything I did. I always operated in a spirit of excellence so I wanted the outcome of everything I was involved in and with to reflect that. I was being led by past behaviors and experiences instead of approaching things with a new set of eyes. I was placing undue and extreme amounts of pressure upon myself. Ultimately, I became concerned about not passing this fear and critical spirit of expectation onto my children.

I am sure everyone has faced or encountered fear at some point in their life. It may show up in different forms such as fear of the unknown, fear of lack, losing control, being alone, or fear of making mistakes. There is no quick remedy for it. Personally, I had to acknowledge it and be courageous enough to deal with it and even through fear pursue my dreams and goals. Take risk!

Maybe it's just me but this is how I used to operate. I would talk myself out of something before I talked myself into it. I would then talk to a few people and get their opinion which I had hoped would help me either continue or decide differently. People advise you based on their experiences and perspective. That's why I said earlier, what I learn in life will impact those connected to me directly or indirectly because I can only share what I know based on knowledge, facts or experiences:

- **Do not rely on others to give you your vision.** It's not your vision if it is coming from someone else. It is okay to have a thought partner and bounce ideas off of each other but if they are flying the plane for you or steering the ship then it is in their best interest and not yours. Know what your vision is. If you don't fully have it, then at least have some idea of what it is and work through identifying the rest. Don't give someone else a blank piece of paper and request them to write the vision for you. You will end up building their dreams and not your own. Define what your vision is and not how others define it for you. Get a trusted and reliable thought partner who will assist you with working out the kinks to get your vision and strategy mapped out.

- **Do not rely on others to validate you.** You know what you know and if you don't know then figure it out. Don't wait or expect to get a pat on the back or round of applause. You have to do what fulfills you whether others agree with it or not. At the end of the day, you are stuck with you 24 hours a day 7 days a week. Find what brings you peace, contentment, and fulfillment in your life and pursue those things.

- **Face your fears.** I could write a few books on fear. I promise you I can. I am more conscious and intentional in doing something that puts me in a position to have to face and overcome my fears. People often tell me how they enjoyed reading my book or they enjoyed hearing me speak somewhere. I did it all with fear. I was afraid but I did it anyway. The more you do it, the less burdensome it is and the more manageable it becomes. Fear could be something we make up in our head about how bad something will be but in reality, once we give it a go or complete it, we see it wasn't that bad after all.

If fear is something you struggle with, take some time (a week or two) and purposely pay attention to your thoughts, feelings and interactions you have in which you experience the emotion of fear. Keep a journal. See if you can identify any patterns. Do you experience fear only in certain situations or with certain people? Recognizing fear is the first step because once you recognize it, you can then decide how you will react to it. Because you feel it does not mean you have to become victim to it. I constantly remind myself while I am doing something that brings fear up in me....*God did not give me a spirit of fear but of power, love, and a sound mind (2 Timothy 1:7).* Face your fears and they will disappear. My youngest told me that. I am never too old to learn from even those younger than me. It's not to say that I don't experience fear. I do but I have learned to not allow the fear to take me off course. Its not to say you won't still be afraid when attempting to do something but should the fear creep in, remind yourself that if you did it once before, you could certainly do it again. Do it.... afraid!

- **Dream big.** Your outlook should be there is no limitation in what you can do. If there is a will then there is a way and if the door won't open, climb through the window or create the door of opportunity. I have seen people grind for years trying to make things happen. I have seen people start out, catch a break and they are hundreds of steps ahead. Besides, there is no timetable that clearly defines how long it should take to reach success or how long it should take to launch a business or how long it should take to complete your degree. In some cases, there are guesstimates and approximations, but they are not clearly outlined as definitive. For instance, when pursuing a degree right after high school, if you are going for an Associate Degree, it could take approximately two years if you attend full time. However, suppose you change your major or change schools and all of your credits are not transferable. The time it takes to complete the two-year degree would be longer. Let's say someone starts and then goes full time with a fall, spring and summer course load. They could potentially complete the degree in slightly under two years. There is no time limit on how you dream. Your dreams are your dreams. What's wrong with dreaming big? Why not dream big?

Writing a book was a start for me. When I started writing my first book over eight years ago, I did not know it would take me so long to complete it. I started and stopped over and over again. Once I published, I was extremely excited but then I started venturing into other things like creating and selling inspirational merchandise that aligned to my book brand and theme. Now, here I am back at it again with my second book. When I was a child, being an author was not something I aspired to do. Remember I said I wanted to be a teacher. My dreams never died. Even now, there is so much more I want to do and plan to do as long as I have breath in my body. My dreams will only cease when I am no longer breathing to make them into a reality.

IT COMES DOWN TO
ONE SIMPLE THING,
HOW BAD DO YOU
WANT IT?

—SLICKWORDS.COM

YOU DECIDE- HOW BAD DO YOU WANT IT?

Every accomplishment starts with the decision to try.

I had to ask myself this question time and time again. How bad do I want it? If I had no desire, hope or motivation, I would allow the chips to fall as they may with no sense of care or concern. Even though I faced times of uncertainty and some setbacks, I never stopped trying to be a better me – a better wife, mom, daughter, employee, church member, a better friend, business woman and an overall better person. I said better (not perfect). I stopped striving for perfection because there was no such thing as perfect. Running around in circles is my equivalent of trying to strive for perfection. It is a never ending pursuit of something superficial.

I thought if I was perfect or did everything perfectly and in order then my problems would dwindle. I would say all the right things, be around who I thought were the right people and make all the right decisions. I was chasing the idea of perfection but life had to show me different. You can still say all the right things to the right people and make what you feel to be all the right decisions. Your conscious may be a little lighter but being this way does not sway the stars to align in your favor, especially when dealing with people. People will be people and you cannot control how they act and what they do. You can only control your reaction and response to them. Needless to say, I was not perfect. At least not in the way I defined perfection.

Do you want to know when I realized this? I was trying to do it all and be all to everyone I dealt with. I was left feeling overwhelmed, unhappy and angry. I had certain standards and expectations already set up in my head and when I didn't meet them, something (usually me) always suffered. I was hard on myself and spent time trying to justify or correct the wrong which had me feeling like a failure. When you know better you do better.

Once I understood what expectations and sometimes limitations I had placed on myself, I had to get to the root cause in order to change. That was one of my first lessons in F.A.I.L.(First Attempt In Learning). I then became driven by my morals, values, ethics, priorities, conscious and even my gut. I was no longer driven to seek perfection. I wanted to change that bad that I had to realize what was not working for me and do something different which changed my thoughts, behavior and actions. When you want something really bad you will come up with ideas and solutions.

Here is a quick challenge. As you read through some initial questions, see what resonates with you and make note of what you already have and what's missing. From the list you create, you can start to formulate your plan and create a set of next steps to pursue your goals and aspirations.

So I ask you the question, how bad do you want it? If you want a better job, how bad do you want it? Have you updated your resume? Do you have a cover letter? Are you actively seeking work by filling out job applications? Are you letting those within your network know that you are looking for work? Have you brushed up on your skills?

Have you researched the area of work you are interested in? Did you create a LinkedIn account to expand your network? Your network is your networth!

*Notes:*_____

_____

_____

_____

_____

_____

If you want to return to school, how bad do you want it? Have you applied to schools? Did you complete a Free Application for Federal Student Aid (FAFSA)? Did you attend any orientations to learn more about the school and program of study? Did you reach out to any college admissions staff? Did you visit the college, university or trade school of interest to you? Did you talk to people who are already working in that particular field just to get an understanding of what the "work" is actually like. Or, did you get their opinion and perspective on their career pathway?

*Notes:*_____

_____

_____

_____

_____

_____

If you want to start a business, how bad do you want it? Have you researched products and services? Do you know what type of business you want to create? Did you complete your business plan? Have you decided on a business name? Have you informed your network of your new business venture? Do you know your target audience? Do you know how you will market your products or services? Have you researched wholesalers? Do you have business cards? Do you have a website or ways for potential customers to contact you? Is there a startup cost? If so, do you have the money or resources to get it? Do you have an elevator pitch? Do you believe in your product or service?

Notes:_____
_____
_____
_____
_____

If you want to write a book, how bad do you want it? Have you started putting your words on paper? Have you decided what type of book you would like to write? Do you have a title? An outline? Do you have an editor or will you edit your own manuscript? *I highly suggest an editor because this is their area of expertise.* Do you have someone to design your book cover? Will you self-publish or seek a publishing company? How will you market and sell your books?

Notes:_____
_____
_____
_____
_____

Even with a goal you need a plan and a strategy to achieve the goal. How bad do you want it? It may take some sleepless nights. It might entail some additional revenue and expenses that you did not anticipate. Sometimes you have to spend money to make money. Are you willing to take risks? It may take you losing some friends along the way. How bad do you want it will determine what your next move will be.

After I published my book and started planning my book release party, I ordered a bunch of shirts. I paid to have this company do a quick GoalGetter logo that I could have printed on the tshirts and sweatshirts. Whenever I had a speaking engagement or an opportunity to be a vendor for an event, I would sell my books and my merchandise. I ended up with a low supply of books as they were selling fast but my merchandise was moving slow. I had to ask myself, how bad do I want it?

I was researching and trying to figure out ways to market and sell what I had. I was having contests and giveaways on Facebook. I was donating a book or piece of merchandise to conferences to be used as a giveaway and raffle prizes for exposure and awareness of my brand. I paid for Facebook and Instagram ads. I was using every social media platform I was familiar with to market and sell my merchandise. I was riding around with books and merchandise in my car just in case an opportunity presented itself where someone was interested in making a purchase, I would be ready. This was my way of getting exposure and getting my name out there. People did not know about me unless I was telling them about me. Every time an opportunity presented itself, I was ready to share what I had and what I knew.

I remember someone saying to me that I am always on Facebook and I post all the time. I could have immediately gotten defensive but I didn't. They were absolutely right. I was talking about me as much as I could (*self-promotion*). People were sharing my information and things were buzzing. That's what I wanted and that's what I will continue to do because that's how bad I want it.

Don't be limited by what other people feel and think you should be doing. You can have anything in life if you want it. It's how bad you want it and what are you willing to do to get it. When people brag about all they have, I don't get upset. I get inspired by hearing how other people are excelling and achieving their goals. If they can do it, I can do it too and that inspires and motivates me constantly. I don't need to be jealous and envious over what someone else has. My philosophy has always been, if I want it I will get it. It may take me a little longer. It may take me having to work multiple jobs. It may take me having to learn a new or different set of skills. Long story short, I can get it too. It's how bad I want it that makes all the difference.

If someone has something that you are interested in, learn from them. Time out for hating on each other. Use it as motivation knowing that if they can get it, so can you. You can have your heart's desire. Again, the question is what are you willing to do to get it and how bad do you want it? When you feel yourself stuck in a decision or fear creeping in, ask yourself...**HOW BAD DO I WANT IT?**

Run your race and not someone else's by keeping YOUR vision and goals in front of you. Dream big and keep growing and learning from the good and the not so good. Stay passionate by lighting the fire within and wake up inspired. Every day commit to investing in yourself and controlling your tongue, thoughts, actions, and attitude.

Last but certainly not least, *expect good things*. If you expect little then you will receive little. Every morning I wake up, I pray and intentionally remind myself that something good is going to happen to me today. Even if my day starts off a little rocky, I remind myself that it can only get better. I am intentional and optimistic about shifting my "atmosphere" and my outlook on the day. It keeps me in a better mood.

Just so you know, I do have days when my thoughts drift to the not so great places and experiences that I have had. I may reflect as my mind drifts off but I don't dwell on it. I don't live in that space. Everything happens for a reason. Always remember that. The experiences up until this point have made you into the individual you are today. If you are happy with it, embrace it. And, if you are unhappy with it then change it.

Personally, I am forever grateful and will continuously program and reprogram my mind toward success. You see I said reprogram because there are times when you may need to reprogram your thoughts, actions and behaviors. Input versus output. If you are putting in crap then you will get crap. You will need to reprogram. Don't be concerned with who is ahead of you and please don't settle for anything less than what YOU feel you deserve.

Run your race, learning and growing along the way, so that when the right doors open for you, you are standing there ready, willing and able. Keep in mind, *winners never quit and quitters never win.*

Stay Ready...*Show up and don't forget to Show Out!*

SELF-REFLECTION

SELF-
REFLECTION
EXERCISES

For God hath not given us the spirit of fear, but of power, and of love, and of a sound mind. (2 Timothy 1:7).

Fear comes in many forms. Some have already been referenced previously. Now is the time to give that "fear" an eviction notice. It has to go. Take some time and write a goodbye letter to whatever it is you may be struggling with (fear, doubt, procrastination, shame, etc).

Write down how it made you feel, how you have been hiding and playing "small" because of it. How it has consumed you or how it has stolen enough time away from you. As you write down how it made you feel finish your letter with a plan of what you will be doing going forward.

Here is a short snippet of how my letter would go….

****

Dear Fear of Failure,

Today is the day that I finally get to say goodbye to you. You have been a thorn in my side for many years now. I talked myself out of business ventures and took less risk because of you being that constant nag to me. Somewhere along the way, I believed I couldn't and, therefore, I didn't.

I have played it "safe" because I felt that you were waiting on the other side ready to laugh and mock at my downfall. I know that perfection is an illusion. Mistakes will happen. As long as I learn from them and continue to do and be the best that I can possibly be, then I won't fail. I am striving for progress and not perfection. Life is a journey and it will entail some highs, some lows, some tears, some disappointments and even some triumphs. But I will no longer be controlled by you. And even when those emotions surface, I will make a conscious effort to try and try some more even if I must do things afraid.

Failure will never be an option for me. I am smart. I am brilliant. I deserve the best and nothing less. I will attract
124

everything that is good to me and for me. No weapon formed against me shall prosper. And just in case I fall down seven times, I will be sure to get up eight. Today is a new day and its time I bid you farewell. Goodbye Fear and Hello Destiny.

Sincerely,

Tamara

Goodbye Letter.

Dear _____;

_____

_____

_____

_____

_____

_____

_____

_____

_____

_____

_____

_____

_____

_____

_____

_____

_____

_____

Self-reflection

What are you most proud of?

_____

_____

_____

When you get to a place where you feel like no one can teach you, show you anything or you have peaked in learning, that's when you actually stop learning. We can always learn something from someone else and as long as you can read you can learn anything.

I challenge you. Think of something you have always wanted to do and write it here. I always wanted to...

_____

_____

_____

_____

Now list at least 4 things you can do to learn it.

1._____

2._____

3._____

4._____

Each day, do at least one of the four things referenced above. This will force you to research, talk to people who are currently doing it, and create a plan to achieve it. You will be taking meaningful steps each day in pursuit of accomplishing that which you have set out to do.

ATTITUDE OF GRATITUDE

ATTITUDE OF GRATITUDE EXERCISE

Regardless of how bad things may seem or appear, we have something to be grateful for. Shifting and reprogramming your mindset will change your focus and attitude as you think about things that are positive in order to develop a habit of thankfulness. For me, it changed my mood and entire being. It changed my perspective and allowed me to see the world and people differently. What are you grateful for? See if you can list at least 10 things you are grateful for. Even after you have made your list of 10 things, each day put your attitude of gratitude into practice by acknowledging something you are grateful for.

1._____

2. _____

3. _____

4. _____

5. _____

6. _____

7. _____

8. _____

9. _____

10. _____

Here is my list. My list does change. I am grateful for:

1. My relationship with God;
2. My husband and our children;
3. My family and circle of friends;
4. Having the courage to write a letter to my fear
5. Being a member of Delta Sigma Theta Sorority Incorporated;
6. Completing my second book;
7. Increasing my credit score;
8. Ability to bounce back after a divorce
9. Having food to cook and eat; and
10. The month of June because I enjoy the summer moreso than winter.

I pray that whenever you experience difficulties or need some encouragement, you will grab and focus on your gratitude list to find assurance, strength and the ability to redirect your thoughts.

Remember to….

"

START EACH DAY WITH AN ATTITUDE OF GRATITUDE

~KEITH HARRELL

ACKNOWLEDGEMENTS

I must first acknowledge my Lord and Savior. Thank you for the constant reminder that I am fearfully and wonderfully made and there is no other person in this entire universe like me. I am one of a kind. Thank you for never leaving me nor forsaking me. For giving me the extra push when you see me becoming complacent. You have shown me over and over again that you got me and always pull me through. Thank you!

To my daughters, you are the wind beneath my wings. God's gift to me was the two of you. You both make me happy and proud to call you my daughters. My words of advice: discover your gifts and talents, don't be afraid to take risks, keep yourself as a priority, DREAM BIG, and always, always look out for each other.

To my bonus children, family is not solely defined by blood relation. Family consists of people you confide in and trust, love and support; through ups, downs, peaks and valleys. I am most grateful to call you my children. I love you all....MY family. Never forget that!

To my brother, you have grown tremendously in the past few years. I am watching you and counting on you to remain true to yourself. You have made it through some tough times. Even when and if you feel like giving up, think about me, mommy, your children, your family on the sidelines with pom poms. We are cheering you on.

To my husband, You have held my hand, had my back, dried my tears and built me up during times when I felt down and most vulnerable. You never cease to amaze me. It hasn't always been easy, but it has been worth it. The past several years have been the best years of my life. Good, bad or indifferent…. You are my Mr. Sunshine!

To my Reader….last but certainly not least!. THANK YOU for buying this book and allowing me to partner and share with you through my personal stories of challenges and triumphs. I encourage you to get serious about your dream, be specific about what you want to achieve, let go of the need for perfection, and allow yourself the liberty to make mistakes. Don't let fear sidetrack you from reaching your destiny. Wave Goodbye to Fear and scream Hello to Destiny!

ABOUT THE AUTHOR

Tamara Mitchell-Davis, born and raised in Hartford, CT, is the Founder and Owner of TM Davis Enterprise LLC. She is a wife, mother, entrepreneur, speaker, life coach and author having released her very first book titled: #GoalGetter: Strategies for Overcoming Life's Challenges (April 2017).

She holds a Master's Degree in Business Administration (MBA), 085 School Business Administrator Certification and a professorial position within the community college system. She teaches business courses on-campus, online and within the Department of Corrections.

She has received various accolades from her community including being honored amongst *100 Women of Color* for leadership and community service. She was also recognized and featured in *Women of Distinction Magazine* as a leader in her field as well as other magazine platforms: *SwagHer Magazine, STS Branding Magazine, DSE Magazine (Winter 2017 edition),* and the *African American Book Festival* author spotlight feature.

In addition, she has appeared on television and radio interview platforms such as *Shine Your Light Radio, Hot 93.7, Qute 89.9 FM,* and *Hartford Public Access Television,* to name a few.

Tamara is a member of Delta Sigma Theta Sorority Incorporated. She spends her time volunteering and fundraising for various organizations near and dear to her heart such as Juvenile Diabetes and the fight against Cancer. She resides in her hometown with her husband Joseph and their children.

TMDAVIS
ENTERPRISE